PUBLIC UTILITIES
AND THE POOR

PUBLIC UTILITIES AND THE POOR

Rights and Responsibilities

DAVID C. SWEET
and
KATHRYN WERTHEIM HEXTER

PRAEGER

New York
Westport, Connecticut
London

Library of Congress Cataloging-in-Publication Data

Sweet, David C.
  Public utilities and the poor.

  Bibliography: p.
  Includes index.
    1. Economic assistance, Domestic—United States.
  2. Poor—United States—Energy assistance.   3. Telephone—
  United States—Rates.   I. Hexter, Kathryn Wertheim.
  II. Title.
  HC110.P6S894   1987   362.5′82   87-6979
  ISBN 0-275-92572-2 (alk. paper)

Library of Congress Catalog Card Number: 87-6979
ISBN:0-275-92572-2

First published in 1987

Praeger Publishers, One Madison Avenue, New York, NY 10010
A division of Greenwood Press, Inc.

Printed in the United States of America

The paper used in this book complies with the
Permanent Paper Standard issued by the National
Information Standards Organization (Z39.48-1984).

10 9 8 7 6 5 4 3 2 1

To

John J. Gilligan

who, during service as city councilman, congressman, governor and federal official, articulated the need for policies and implemented programs related to those of lesser means in our society,

who, in perhaps his highest calling as professor, shares his commitment to and concern for the public service obligation we all share, and

who provided me the opportunity to test ideas and concepts in the real world, thereby gaining experiences, insights, and friendships of an everlasting nature.

D.C.S.

Contents

List of Tables and Figures   ix
Foreword by Dennis E. Eckart   xi
Foreword by J. Richard Kelso   xv
Preface   xvii
Introduction   xxi

Part I   ENERGY AND THE POOR   1

1   The Nature of Energy Assistance Programs   3
2   The Emergence of the First Crisis: Energy for Heating   7
3   Energy and Cities   25

PART II   THE PUBLIC SECTOR RESPONSE   31

4   The Case for Federal Intervention   33
5   The Case for State Intervention   51

PART III   THE PRIVATE AND INDEPENDENT SECTOR RESPONSE   69

6   The Independent Sector Response   71
7   The Case for Utility Leadership   79

PART IV   A NEW CRISIS/A NEW APPROACH   89

8   Telephone Rates and the Poor   91
9   The Policy-Making Process: Lessons Learned   115
10   The Policy-Making Process: A New Era   125

Appendix A: Testimony   143
Appendix B: Summary of FCC-Approved State Lifeline Assistance
              Programs   147
Notes   151
Selected Bibliography   161
Index   165
About the Authors   173

List of Tables and Figures

TABLES

2.1 Estimated National Average Home Energy Costs as a Percent of Income for Selected Years, 1972–81   11

2.2 Estimated National Average Total Energy Costs as a Percent of Income for Selected Years, 1973–80   12

2.3 Average Annual Expenditures for Selected Categories by Quintiles of Income, 1980–81   13

2.4 Average Bill Comparison LIHEAP/PIPP/OEC   16

2.5 Percentage of Households Making Lifestyle Sacrifices and Energy Efficiency Investments, Saint Paul, Minnesota, 1980   20

3.1 Inflation of Selected Components of Housing Costs: A Comparison: 1972, 1978, 1985   26

4.1 U.S. Weatherization Funding and Direct Assistance Funding   41

5.1 State Energy Assistance Programs by Type and Year, 1979, 1981, 1984   52

5.2 1979 Direct Aid Program Components   57

5.3 1981 Direct Aid Program Components   58

5.4 1984 Direct Aid Program Components   59

5.5 Direct Aid Programs—Total State Funding Levels, 1979, 1981, 1984   60

5.6 State Weatherization/Conservation Programs by Type and Year, 1979, 1981, 1984   61

8.1 Development of U.S. Telephone Service   93

8.2 Threats to Universal Service in 1984: The Source of the Problem   95

8.3 Estimated Percentage of Households with Basic Telephone Service   96

8.4 Bell System Subscriber Plant Costs for 1981 and Interstate

Allocation of Subscriber Plant Costs per Subscriber Line
per Month   100
8.5   Lifeline Telephone Service: Initial Federal Proposals   103
8.6   Telephone Rates and the Poor: The State Response   105

FIGURES

8.1   Percent Increase in Energy Prices and Federal Poverty
Threshold, 1973-83   92
8.2   Percentage of Subscriber Plant Costs Allocated to Interstate Service   99
8.3   A Framework for Options: Lifeline Telephone Rates   112
9.1   The Ohio Energy Assistance Quagmire   116
10.1 Stakeholder Map of a Telecommunications Firm   131
10.2 Generic Strategies for Stakeholders   133
10.3 The Ohio Energy Assistance Quagmire Simplified by Addition of the One-Stop Outreach, Application, and Information Center   137
10.4 Vendor Line-of-Credit Model   139

Foreword

The Honorable Dennis E. Eckart
Democratic Representative, 11th District, Ohio
U.S. Congress

I first had the opportunity to work closely with David Sweet in the late 1970s on the development and operation of Ohio's Energy Credits Program. While a member of the Ohio State Legislature, I served as chairman of the Energy Credits Advisory Committee, and we sought and relied upon the special assistance and insight provided to us by Dr. Sweet, one of Ohio's foremost authorities on energy policy. I am, therefore, honored to be a part of this publication which he has co-authored on a subject addressing concerns we share on a local, state, and federal level.

Ohio's Energy Credits Program, providing direct financial assistance to the elderly and poor unable to meet their utility bills, was one of the first such comprehensive state-run programs enacted in the nation. Other efforts have followed, both in our own state and across the country, as the pressing need to resolve the "eating or heating" choice faces many fixed-income families. While innovative and successful programs such as Ohio's Energy Credits Program have undeniably made important strides toward resolving this crisis, our nation clearly needs to reassess how we set utility rates, who ultimately bears the burden for these decisions, and how we can most effectively and efficiently meet the long-term needs of the poor and elderly.

One shortcoming of the federal government, and to a lesser degree of state governments, is its inability to form policies and programs that anticipate, rather than react to, crises and the resulting needs of the people caught up in them. It was the federal government's slow call to action during the energy crisis of the 1970s that prompted Ohio to take matters into its own hands and devise programs to address the rapidly increasing costs of heating and other utility bills. Our state's Low-Income Home Energy Assistance Program (LIHEAP) is another example of a successful effort that nonetheless struggles from year to year to maintain an adequate funding level and increase its effectiveness. Reacting to, rather than anticipating, these needs through a disjointed patchwork of state and federally-controlled programs continues to do little more than apply hastily and inadequately apportioned band-aids to ills far more serious than the remedies acknowledge.

Like most major economic problems confronting our nation, there are no "quick fixes" for resolving the inability of many citizens to keep pace with rising utility costs. As we have learned over the years, direct financial assistance is not a long-term solution. In too many instances, the families requiring help live in buildings in need of modernization and weatherization repairs. Providing them with utility payment assistance without taking steps to correct the structural problems contributing to the size of bills, or without properly informing them about energy conservation methods, is both inefficient and fiscally irresponsible.

The complexity of the problem highlights why it is imperative that solutions be multifaceted, fully involving consumers, utilities, private enterprise, and local, state, and federal governments. The federal government on its own has had difficulty in implementing this type of integrated approach. The very nature of our government's structure tends to preclude the formation of programs drawing upon the support and cooperation of several sectors and disciplines.

As a member of the House Energy and Commerce Committee, I will be playing an active role during the 100th Congress in the formation of new telecommunications policies demanded by the rapid pace of growth and change in this industry. Undoubtedly, rising telephone rates and questions about universal access to telecommunications innovations will be receiving national attention.

In the state Legislature in the 1970s, I moved foward in developing "911" Emergency telephone network legislation and devised legislative methods to avoid shifting higher costs to residential consumers through so-called "lifeline" phone rates. I continue this interest in Washington as affordable and available telephone service, while not as emotional a need as heat or electricity, is a service which all consumers deserve and upon which many rely for health and safety needs. To be truly effective, our efforts to address these needs must again rely on a network of assistance and input. As with all utilities, the involvement of the telephone companies in the formation of consumer-oriented policies and programs ultimately serves their own best business and social interests. All stakeholders have a critical role to play, and without any one of the integrated components, the effort may fail.

The role of state Public Utility Commissions has broadened in recent years beyond the original purpose of reviewing and setting rates, and the development of other consumer advocate groups, such as Ohio's Consumer Counsel, ensure better representation of consumers' interests in utility rate matters. All these components are now beginning to mesh into an effort to further define the responsibilities of public utilities to help the poor. The messages shared through this book are timely indeed, coming to us just as we have enough history from which to draw solid conclusions, and while there is clearly still a great need for action and change.

Foreword

J. Richard Kelso, President
East Ohio Gas Company
Cleveland, Ohio

The high public profile projected by this nation's energy utility suppliers reflects the importance energy plays in our lives. Our businesses, our homes, our schools—virtually every facet of life is affected by the availability and price of energy.

In recent years it has become increasingly clear that the earth's energy resources are not finite; nor are those remaining resources inexpensive to procure.

As a result, even the industry's successful efforts to stabilize the price of natural gas have not been able to fully shield consumers from a rise in the price of energy.

For that reason, the companies that produce, supply and distribute energy no longer view their operations simply as a business, but as a commitment to those they serve—the poor as well as the affluent.

I am proud that the company I represent has been a key player in the development of state and local programs to help the poor and elderly maintain their energy services. Ohio Energy Credits, Weatherization and the People-Helping-People Fuel Fund are but a few of the programs developed through the joint efforts of the local utilities such as East Ohio, local and state government, consumer organizations and other stakeholders.

Dr. Sweet and Ms. Hexter, in writing this book, have completed a painstaking and important task. As a corporate executive, I have found that one of the most important management tools is listening, and this book has much to say to us. It neither glosses over mistakes nor aggrandizes successes.

It points up, rather, the serious work we have before us, and points to ways that can help assure adequate public utility service for the poor. *Public Utilities and the Poor* is a document that should be on the "must read" list of all who have a stake in attaining that goal.

Preface

The initial concept for this book emerged while wrestling with the turbulent set of energy policy issues as a state official in the 1970s. It was refined upon becoming a university dean and professor, as a result of research undertaken with the support of a series of grants. And finally, *Public Utilities and the Poor: Rights and Responsibilities* was written with a college colleague, Kathryn Wertheim Hexter, who subsequently became a community service representative for a gas utility company.

As a result, the book spans a decade of development in the energy policy arenas at the federal, state and local level—a period of time which featured dramatic increases in energy costs, policy debates and conflicts among utility regulators, utility executives, state and federal lawmakers, and a variety of other stakeholders—most notably the low and fixed income households confronted with paying their utility bills.

While the authors take full responsibility for the content and recommendations developed in the book, the concepts which have been defined owe their shaping to interaction with many individuals, as well as funding support from a few, who had the foresight to anticipate the inevitable emergence of this issue as a key component in the overall energy policy debates. Recognizing the inevitable problem of singling out a few, and potentially offending many, who have contributed ideas and suggestions along the way, with our apologies to the latter group, we indicate our appreciation to those without whose support this book would not have been possible.

Congressman Dennis Eckart, while serving in the Ohio legislature and chairing a committee evaluating the Ohio Energy Credits program, provided the first grant to a newly appointed college dean which led to the initial survey of the fifty states and their response to the issue of energy and the poor. Tom Conlan and Sara Larson were there at the start as staff to the committee.

Howard Perry of the U.S. Department of Energy, William C. Pendleton of the Ford Foundation, Charles T. Caprino of the Connecticut Department of Public Utility Control, and C. Kenneth Orski of the German Marshall Fund were early supporters of grant projects that evaluated alternative policy options being undertaken at the state and local level to aid low and fixed income households in confronting rising energy costs.

Subsequent funding for evaluation and demonstration projects undertaken by the College of Urban Affairs has been provided by The Standard Oil Company's Office of Corporate Contributions (C. Lance Buhl), The Cleveland Foundation (Steven A. Minter), the George Gund Foundation (Daniel Berry), the Ohio Department of Development (William Whitney) and the Ohio Public Utilities Commission (Thomas Chema).

Carol Werner, long an advocate of low-income energy assistance, first with the National Consumer Law Center and now with the Northeast-Midwest Institute, provided invaluable advice and counsel.

Along with documenting the emergence of a variety of policy options, the book advocates a new, for many, management approach for utility or program administrators. This approach, stakeholder management, has long been incorporated in some successful utility organizations. However, Maurice MacCarthy has been its most ardent disciple, and in his role as training coordinator for AT&T and most recently director of training for BellCor Tech-East has conveyed the concepts to thousands of telephone company middle and senior managers. R. Edward Freeman, Professor of Business Administration at the University of Virginia, has written and lectured extensively on stakeholder management concepts and practices. The interaction with these two while developing a series of invited lectures on state regulatory policies has been an invaluable experience for me in expanding and shaping the concept of stakeholder management in the public policy arena.

Long before I had read of the concept, Jack I. Criswell, now retired from Ohio Bell Telephone, provided a fine example of stakeholder management in action and William (Gus) Gustaferro as Senior Vice President of Ohio Bell Telephone has provided valuable insights and interactions from a senior utility manager's perspective, along with a critique of the book's concluding chapters. These individuals, along with Francis Wright, retired president of East Ohio Gas Company, and current president, J. Richard Kelso, provide models for corporate leadership in an era of dramatic change in the utility business.

Finally and perhaps foremost, are a group of colleagues at Cleveland State University who have assisted in many ways. Linda L. Berger provided early research assistance for the book. Professor Edric A. Weld completed the first nationwide survey of state programs with the assistance of Jean Standish, who subsequently has directed two additional national surveys of programs. Dr. Thomas P. Pelsoci headed several of the major grant projects, David F. Garrison, Director of the College's Urban Center, and Professor Norman

Krumholz, who heads the Neighborhood Development Center, have guided the energy program work as a central part of our neighborhood technical assistance efforts. Suzanne Hartman, Linda Keegan, and Kenneth Martau have helped in moving the project to completion. Kathy Kukuca, Joy Walworth and Dr. Seymour Goldstone provided valuable editorial critiques and assistance. Mary Helen Kelly has kept track of a decade's worth of project correspondence, drafts and related material and Sondra Steele did yeoman's service in entering, correcting and printing the numerous drafts that have been completed in the course of this effort. To all we say a sincere thank you.

Introduction

In 1972 when energy prices in the United States were relatively low and energy supplies were virtually uninterrupted, energy assistance for low-income and elderly households was not an issue. In 1973, the Organization of Petroleum Exporting Countries (OPEC) limited the flow of oil to the United States. Prices rose. Beginning in 1974, energy assistance gradually emerged as a pressing national concern.

Spiraling U.S. energy prices forced all Americans to rethink consumption habits and spending patterns. Households adjusted life-styles, turned down thermostats, and adopted a more responsible waste-not attitude toward (energy) usage. Even as prices began to plateau, the effects were still being felt at all economic levels of society. A low-cost, uninterrupted supply of energy would never again be taken for granted.

While all Americans felt the immediate impact of OPEC's 1973 oil embargo, none felt it as immediately or as pervasively as those who lacked the resources to respond—those living on low and fixed incomes. The national movement toward energy independence spawned by the OPEC embargo captured the limelight as energy policy experts debated and discussed pricing mechanisms and other policy issues.

Long functioning in the background, state public utility commissions were thrust into the public eye and became highly controversial. Rate increases granted to keep utilities financially healthy contrasted with demands for consumer rate relief. Community Action Agencies, which had a history of addressing community concerns, and other local social service agencies struggled with new concerns related to energy and the poor. Consumer advocates and local government officials intervened in utility rate cases on behalf of their beleaguered constituents.

If the price to be paid for our increased national energy independence was higher cost, social policy experts argued that programs were needed to mitigate the effects of this policy on the nation's poor.

In 1977 the nation was hit again—this time by a shortage of natural gas. Schools and offices closed. People were urged to turn down their themostats. The Department of Energy was established. President Carter made energy assistance a focus of national energy policy in his first National Energy Plan, declaring: "In particular, the elderly, the poor, and those on fixed incomes, should be protected from disproportionately adverse effects on their income. Energy is as necessary to life as food and shelter."[1]

In the following decade, hundreds of national, state, and local programs were developed to address energy assistance for the poor. Volumes of books and reports were written and numerous discussions were held on the topic and billions of federal, state, local, and private dollars were spent in an effort to protect the poor from the disproportionate effects of rising energy prices.

Yet near the end of the decade of the oil embargo that sent energy prices in the United States skyrocketing, the goal of protecting the poor (from disproportionately adverse effects) remained elusive. Senator Edward M. Kennedy called the lack of effective, long-term solutions to this problem "the greatest failure of our nation's energy policy."[2]

Little was known about the relationship between energy and the poor when the first energy programs began. This lack of knowledge and the lack of a careful, studied approach were significant barriers to the development of effective programs. For example, a program centered on conservation seemed the most sound policy because improved residential energy efficiency leads to lower consumption, reducing demand for more costly direct assistance programs, that is, payment of utility bills. Yet politics dictated that immediate needs be met as images of the elderly, huddled in freezing homes, permeated the media.

Energy assistance began as a solution to what many thought was a temporary crisis. However, when the crisis became a long-term problem, the type of assistance available did not change accordingly.

In their well-intentioned search for answers, federal, state, and local governments created an overlapping and conflicting programmatic morass. This not only made it more difficult for the poor and elderly to access and use these programs, but also prevented those interested in improving the delivery of assistance from addressing the problems in delivery and consequently from making the programs more responsive to the needs of the poor and elderly. Sheer complexity insulated the programs from the people they were intended to serve.

In confronting issues of this type, policy makers must answer several questions. How can a problem of this magnitude, with life-threatening consequences for those in need, be allowed to develop and continue? How can our governing bodies expend such a large portion of their resources and do no more than scratch the surface? This book will focus on the barriers to equitable, efficient, and effectively designed programs related to the issue of public utilities and the poor and will discuss alternative policy approaches to overcoming these barriers, approaches that can be initiated in both the public and private sectors.

The energy assistance problem caused by the dramatic escalation in energy costs is illustrative of the many structural problems confronting the poor. As we have not yet developed a successful approach to dealing with these structural problems, it is hardly surprising that the energy assistance problem has not been adequately addressed.

In the wake of the recent divestiture of the American Telephone and Telegraph Company, many analysts are predicting a dramatic increase in the costs of local telephone service similar to that in the cost of energy. What lessons can be learned from the efforts of government and business to resolve the energy assistance problem? How can the various stakeholders concerned about *rights* of the individual consumers and the companies who provide the services as well as their individual *responsibilities* work together in addressing these critical issues?

These are the issues that will be explored in the following chapters. Parts I, II, and III trace the evolution of energy assistance policy in the United States from the early 1970s to the present. The roles of the public and private sectors are examined in defining the issues and funding, designing, and implementing programs. Part I describes the nature of the problem. Part II discusses the roles and responsibilities of federal, state, and local governments. Part III describes the role of the private and independent sectors—utility companies, foundations, and corporations. The public sector has a strong, central role to play. The federal government's role is to equalize the impact of policies and programs that led to increased energy prices by guaranteeing a minimum level of assistance across states through funding and guidelines. State and, to a lesser extent, local governments are in the best position to design programs to use this money to their best advantage within federal guidelines and to augment the federal dollars as needed.

The private sector's role is to add the highlights to the energy assistance picture. Utility companies and corporate and community foundations can develop programs that meet specific local needs and pilot innovative solutions to the problem.

Part IV discusses the "emerging crisis" in the public utility area: telephone rates and the poor. Chapter 9 identifies the lessons learned during the past decade of energy assistance policy making and discusses their implications for future policies. Chapter 10 discusses the era of "New Federalism" and its implication for those concerned with the issue of public utilities and the poor, describes an alternative approach to the adversarial approach to policy making (which was prescribed in the past) and finally suggests several improved policy directions.

PART I

ENERGY AND THE POOR

1

The Nature of Energy Assistance Programs

The cost of energy poses a unique challenge to the poor. During the 1970s the rise in energy costs confronted all households regardless of income. This created a widespread empathy—particularly with those living just above the poverty line, the elderly and working poor, the "deserving poor"—and an equally widespread willingness to assist those least able to absorb the rising prices. Consequently, politically powerful interests that might oppose increases in AFDC (Aid to Families with Dependent Children) or food stamp programs were more tolerant of the concept of energy assistance.

Energy assistance programs were born through the efforts of a broad constituency because the problem of energy and the poor occupies a multidimensional universe. It reflects a housing problem, an income problem, a credit problem, a legal problem, and an energy conservation problem. It directly affects a variety of unaligned stakeholders and interests that include the elderly, the poor, utilities and their stockholders, fuel oil dealers, consumer advocates, government officials, and social service agencies—each with a different perspective and a different stake.

Yet this broad constituency failed to define a common ground and, as a result, has generated a complex energy assistance bureaucracy that now is an intractable part of the system. Turf protection often overrides other concerns, much to the detriment of the low-income household. In many cases programs have developed their own zealous constituencies that—at the minimum—seek to sustain the status quo. Program objectives (if indeed they ever existed) are forgotten in the infighting and confusion.

There are three basic approaches to providing energy assistance to the poor: (1) energy conservation/weatherization, (2) direct financial assistance, and (3) rate relief or rate reform. President Carter's comprehensive energy program of 1979 was based on the premise that energy conservation should be the heart of a national effort to achieve energy security; he described it as "the quickest, cheapest, cleanest way to reduce our dependence on foreign oil."[1]

Mr. Carter's program recognized the adverse impacts energy conservation could have on different segments of society and tried to use energy assistance as compensation. His goals in energy assistance, however, were often conflicting and unclear:

1. To protect the elderly, the poor, and those on fixed incomes from disproportionately adverse effects on their income;
2. To reduce our dependence on foreign oil; and
3. To train and employ the underemployed.

The Reagan administration approached energy policy quite differently. The "New Federalism," Reagan's movement toward decentralization, shifted the responsibility for energy assistance to state and local governments and to the private sector without regard to the inequities between energy-rich and energy-poor states.

The downplaying of the federal role in energy assistance came at a time when the need for assistance was on the rise as a result of recession-related high levels of unemployment and cuts in other federal programs for the poor. To further compound the problem, the real income of low-income households was falling, affecting individual households' cash flow. Also deeply affected was the cash flow of those states in the "frost belt," the largest energy importers and consumers.

Given the virtual certainty of an increasing energy cost burden on all households and the likelihood of federal, state, and local funding reductions, what can be done to help those most in need cope with energy costs? Under the Reagan administration the responsibility for answering this question has been effectively shifted to the state and local levels—the state level because Reagan's block grants give the states the responsibility for deciding what kind of energy assistance is provided with federal funding, who is eligible for it, and how it is delivered; and the local level because individuals turn first to local leaders in crisis situations, expecting clarity and coordination to be drawn by them from the multitude of energy assistance programs. While states, local governments, and the private sector have demonstrated their capacity to develop creative and effective programs to address energy assistance needs, in most cases these are on a small scale. They do not have the revenue sources of the federal government, nor do they have broad powers to address issues that cross state lines or demand resolution at a national level.

In 1980 the Department of Energy's Fuel Oil Marketing Advisory Committee (FOMAC) estimated that an effective national energy assistance program would cost $4.5 billion for the fiscal year (FY) 1981 winter heating season. Yet the federal energy assistance appropriation was only $1.85 billion for that winter and $1.87 billion for the winter of 1982. Increases in program funding through FY 1985 were marginal. Even though some states were contributing their own funds to supplement the federal dollars, the total amounts fell far short of meeting the need. The record for weatherization assistance is equally grim. The Bureau of the Census and the Department of Energy (DOE) indicate approximately 12.6 million households in the country are eligible for weatherization assistance. By FY 1986, approximately 1.5 million households will have been weatherized by the DOE weatherization assistance program. At the proposed FY 1986 funding level of $152.9 million, 148,000 homes could be weatherized per year. At that rate, it would take 75 years to weatherize all eligible homes.

It is ironic that as the challenges confronting state and local governments increase and their ability to improve access to services improves, the financial resources to enable them to meet these challenges are threatened by budget cuts. The New Federalism failed to yield the revenue sources necessary for state and local governments to carry out their new program responsibilities. The music simply stopped; states were on their own.

The crisis orientation of energy assistance programs changed little in their first decade despite the changing needs and politics. As early as 1979, there was a general consensus that programs should offer at least the following elements:

1. Direct financial assistance to those least able to bear the rising costs of energy and/or least able to adjust their consumption downward;
2. Effective weatherization programs to assist low-income households to reduce their need for energy during the heating season; and
3. Load-management programs applicable to industrial and commercial as well as residential customers to reduce peak demand for energy and therefore slow down the need for expensive construction and on-line maintenance of new capacity.

But the bulk of federal funds flowed to direct assistance because of the urgent needs in that area.

There was also a consensus on the need for coordination among programs. A survey of state-initiated energy assistance programs conducted by Cleveland State University in 1979[2] found that coordination was needed at two levels: policy-making and service-delivery. The Cleveland State University study called for a major reassessment of residential energy policy on a state-by-state basis as well as a national basis. In spite of this and other similar recommendations, coordination efforts at the state level met with only limited success.

What was then found to be true is even more true today. Nearly all of the 100-plus energy assistance programs examined in the original survey dealt with only one facet of the energy situation. Most were compensatory, attempting to offset the effects of rising energy costs, rather than to help people deal more effectively with the changes under way.

It was suggested that states reassess the whole range of policies relating to residential energy usage in response to the changes that occurred in federal regulations, energy-saving technology, and knowledge of improved delivery systems (such as energy audits). An update of this survey revealed that the states and the federal government have yet to undertake this reassessment.[3]

If state and local governments are to be successful in defining and carrying out their role in the New Federalism's realignment of responsibility, it is necessary to develop strategies that address the needs of their individual states and localities within the broader context of federal energy policies. However, the different components of the energy assistance problem must be identified and understood before effective strategies can be developed. Common areas of interest among the divergent groups of consumers, utilities, corporations, stockholders, senior citizens, manufacturers, welfare rights organizations, and others with a stake in the outcome of energy assistance programs must be developed. The first step in solving the energy assistance crisis is to define the problem.

2

The Emergence of the First Crisis: Energy For Heating

In the development of energy assistance policy at the federal, state, and local level, it is important to understand how low-income households are affected by, and respond to, rising energy prices. Specifically, two questions must be addressed. First, how have rising energy prices affected the ability of low-income households to pay for the energy needed to heat and cool their homes and second, what level of control do these households have over the amount of energy they use in their homes? This chapter will discuss these two issues and the way in which they relate to national income-maintenance and housing policies.

The rapid increases in home energy costs of the early 1970s far outpaced any increase in the level of assistance provided by income-maintenance programs. Tight household budgets were stretched to their limits. Recognizing the impact of these rapid price increases, federal and state governments created energy assistance programs to help people meet the crisis. The first programs were considered temporary crisis-intervention programs that would supplement existing income-maintenance programs, as well as provide some support to those who were newly poor as a result of the sudden increases in energy costs. But income-maintenance programs never caught up with energy-fueled inflation; in fact, the availability of energy assistance funds was later used in many states and at the federal level as a basis for limiting increases in welfare benefit levels. In this context, the way in which poverty is defined in large part determines a household's ability to pay for energy and, therefore, its need for energy assistance programs.

There are two standard measures of low income or poverty that are widely used in the United States. One is the "poverty index." It calculates poverty as a function of the cost of a bare subsistence diet (based on the Department of Agriculture's economy food plan of 1961) and the national average ratio of family food expenditures to total family after-tax income (as measured in the 1955 Household Food Consumption Survey). Basically, any family whose income is less than three times the minimum food budget for the number of persons in that family is considered poor. In 1980, a nonfarm family of four living in Washington, D.C., earning less than $8,450 was considered poor.[1]

A second, more liberal measure of poverty is set by the Department of Labor Bureau of Labor Statistics (BLS).[2] Any household with an annual income less than or equal to 125 percent of the lower-living standard (LLS) determined each year by the secretary of labor is deemed poor. Like the poverty index, the LLS is based on both household size and income. Using the BLS standards an income of $14,044 for a nonfarm family of four is considered poor.[3]

In an analysis of the impact of the rise in energy prices on low-income groups, Lindsay Wright and Loren C. Cox of the MIT Energy Laboratory suggest a third measure of poverty based on their premise that measures based on gross annual income figures may mistake the true earning and spending power of such groups as the self-employed and the temporarily unemployed or underemployed whose income may vary greatly from year to year. Consequently, they suggest other measures, such as a household's purchasing power,[4] or a deprivation index.[5]

Estimates based on 1972–73 BLS expenditure data indicate that families in the lowest decile draw on other resources. These resources are primarily in-kind assistance such as housing assistance, Medicare, Medicaid, and food stamps. They allow these families to spend about 1.5 times their total annual income.[6] They also have inspired the Reagan administration to propose an adjustment to both the poverty index and the BLS standards by counting in-kind benefits as income.

This notion of counting in-kind benefits as income represents an attempt to move away from the traditional definitions of poverty in cash terms. It could lead to many of those now classified as poor being reclassified as non-poor and destined for reductions in benefits.

For example, the Reagan administration's repeated attempts to count energy assistance as income would reduce an AFDC recipient's check one dollar for each dollar of energy assistance and cause a reduction of from $3.50 to $5.25 in food stamps for every $10.00 in energy assistance. Low-Income Home Energy Assistance Program (LIHEAP) recipients are protected by an "income disregard" clause that prohibits the inclusion of LIHEAP benefits in income for the purpose of determining food stamp eligibility and efforts to change this continue to be opposed by consumer groups.

Existing programs are not currently reaching all those eligible for assistance under existing criteria—much less all those in need. Changing definitions of poverty or lowering eligibility requirements may make fewer people eligible but do not change the number of people in need. The experience of energy assistance programs demonstrates that even current measures of poverty alone are not adequate to indicate need for energy assistance. The type of fuel used, the degree-days, and the age and condition of the housing stock are additional factors that must be considered with income to determine a household's ability to pay for its needed energy. (Degree-days: The sum over a representative calendar year of the absolute difference between each day's average temperature and 65 degrees. The higher an area's degree days, the greater the area's heating and cooling energy requirement.)

There is a significant class of households not considered poor even under the standard pre-Reagan definitions of poverty that obviously need energy assistance. These households are predominantly elderly and live on fixed or limited incomes. Typically they worked all their lives, paid off their home mortgages, and live on Social Security, perhaps augmented by small savings or a pension. Before the rapid increase in energy prices they managed, barely, to keep up with expenses by carefully budgeting resources. With the exception of Medicare/Medicaid they receive no form of public assistance and would rather do without than live on the dole.

A letter from Ohioan Elsie Gerbhardt to her state's then-Governor James Rhodes poignantly summarizes their burden under rising utility prices:

I am 84 years old and retired and I have a sister Amelia Gerbhardt, her age is 94 years old and all our lives we have deprived ourselves of a lot just so when we got older we could pay our bills and now we have to use our savings to pay bills to heat our home. In December 1975, my gas bill was $48.04, then in January 1977 I paid $275.10. . . . We just took our savings and paid our bills but it did hurt . . . isn't there anything you can do for senior citizens at our ages?[7]

There are many like Elsie Gerbhardt not included in standard definitions of poverty and unlikely to apply for assistance even though they are desperately in need.

Determining who stands on which side of the poverty line does not complete the picture of the need for energy assistance. It is also important to determine a household's capacity to respond to rising energy prices or, in economic terms, the price elasticity of the poor's demand for energy.

Since the early 1970s many studies have been done that attempt to document the level of need, and much progress has been made in identifying the impact of energy price increases on the poor. However, the findings of these studies vary widely, depending on the methodology used; different definitions of poverty and the way in which the problem is defined yield different results. Some researchers examined the impact of total home energy consumption, including gasoline costs, while others looked only at heating and cooling. Still others included indirect energy costs, which are the costs of the energy consumed in the manufacture, production, or delivery of purchased goods and services.

Another difficulty in evaluating home energy consumption is that it is highly individualized and varies depending on geographic region, fuel source, weather, and personal habits and routines. The lack of uniform data meant studies could not be compared over time.

From 1978–1979, the Department of Energy began to collect uniform information about energy costs, consumption patterns, and conservation through its Residential Energy Consumption Survey. Policy seemed to be more firmly based.

However, even the most well-designed study cannot completely explain energy consumption patterns because of highly individualized variations in consumption within regions and among different classes of households caused by differing fuel sources, weather, and personal habits and routines.

These early studies[8] have led policy makers to base decisions on the following premises regarding energy and the poor: (1) low and fixed-income households paid and continue to pay a higher portion of their income on energy than other income groups; (2) they experience a household budget crunch because of inflation assumed to be fueled by high energy costs; (3) they use less energy than higher income households; and (4) they have limited capacity to respond to rising prices through conservation measures or substitute fuels. Each premise is examined in greater detail below.

DO THE POOR PAY MORE?

Based on the different definitions of poverty discussed above, household energy costs can be looked at in two ways: first in relation to income and second in relation to expenditures. Most existing studies use income as the basis for determining whether the poor pay more for energy. The cost of home energy for different income groups as a percent of income is compared in Table 2.1. The cost of total energy, including gasoline costs, is compared in Table 2.2.

There is some difficulty in making comparisons across studies stemming from the different definitions of "low" and "moderate" income and the different methodologies used in obtaining data. However, it is possible to identify a range of the relative amount of income spent on energy over time. As Tables 2.1 and 2.2 illustrate, the segment of household income apportioned to energy costs increased for all income groups since 1973, but the proportion of the low-income household's income apportioned to energy costs rose at a higher rate (from 1.2 to 2.8 times higher, depending on the study).

Home energy expenditures take from 4 to 6 times as much of the average low-income household's income as of the median-income household's income, again depending on the study.

When gasoline costs are included, this differential decreases to 2.7 times the proportion of income. This suggests that for lower-income households,

Table 2.1

Estimated National Average Home Energy Costs as a Percent of Income for Selected Years, 1972–81

Study	Year	Income		
		Low (less than $5,000)	Lower Middle ($5,000 - $9,999)	Non-Lower ($10,000 +)
Cooper, Sullivan[1] et al.	1972-73	11.0%	5.2%	2.5%
	1979-80	21.1	8.9	3.5
	1980-81	23.2	9.7	3.5

Study	Year	Income			
		Low Income		Median Income	
		Average Income Level	% Spent on Energy	Average Income Level	% Spent on Energy
FOMAC[2]	1978	$3,401	17.8%	$17,640	4.3%
	1979	3,549	19.7	18,825	4.7
	1980	3,703	21.8	20,196	5.1

[1]*Source:* Mark N. Cooper, Theodore L. Sullivan, Susan Punnett, and Ellen Berman, *Equity and Energy: Rising Energy Prices and the Living Standards of Lower Income Americans* (Boulder, Colorado: Westview Press, 1983), p. 82. Reprinted with permission.

[2]*Source:* U.S. Department of Energy, Fuel Oil Marketing Advisory Committee (FOMAC), *Low-Income Energy Assistance Programs: A Profile of Need and Policy Options* (Washington, D.C., July 1980), p. 10.

home energy costs are a much larger proportion of their total energy costs than for the upper-income household, which tends to spend more discretionary money on gasoline.

An examination of household expenditures, based on the BLS 1980–81 Consumer Expenditure Survey (See Table 2.3), shows that the average low-income household (income under $3,473 per annum) spent 1.7 times its income on such necessities as food, shelter, fuels, telephone, water and public services, transportation and health care. This suggests that in-kind assistance is a significant part of its budget. The average moderate-income household (income of approximately $10,000 per annum) and the average median-income household (income of about $20,000 per annum) spent 85 percent and 57.2 percent of their incomes on these items, respectively.

The relative rank of expenditures for these items indicates that food, shelter, and transportation took the largest proportion of the low-income household's total expenditures at 23.2, 19.4, and 15.9 percent, respectively. Health care costs ranked fourth, followed very closely by fuel costs at 5.9 percent. Telephone service ranked sixth, followed by other utilities. Similar spending patterns are exhibited by the two other income groups examined (see Table 2.3).

When fuel expenditures are examined in relation to total household ex-

Table 2.2

Estimated National Average Total Energy Costs* as a Percent of Income for Selected Years, 1973–80

Study	Year	Low Income		Median Income	
		Average Income Level	% Spent on Energy	Average Income Level	% Spent on Energy
Newman & Day	1972-1973	$2,500	15.2%	$14,000	5.9%
FOMAC	1978	3,401	24.5	17,640	9.5
FOMAC	1979	3,549	29.5	18,825	11.2
FOMAC	1980	3,703	35.7	20,196	13.2

*Includes natural gas, electricity and gasoline.

Sources: Dorothy K. Newman and Dawn Day, *The American Energy Consumer* (Cambridge: Ballinger Publishing Co., 1975), p. 116, Table 5-27. U.S. Department of Energy, Fuel Oil Marketing Advisory Committee (FOMAC), *Low-Income Energy Assistance Programs: A Profile of Need and Policy Options,* July 1980, p. 9. Reprinted with permission of the Washington Research Center—formerly Washington Center for Metropolitan Studies.

penditures, low-income households spend only a slightly higher proportion than moderate- and median-income households.

Getting back to the original question, "Do the Poor Pay More?" this analysis concludes that in relative terms the poor do pay more. In relation to their income, they pay much more. In relation to total expenditures, they pay only slightly more. This suggests that increases in energy prices since 1972 have increased the dependency of the lowest income households on government assistance programs to fill the income/expenditure gap. Low-income households had no discretionary cushion to absorb the larger bite taken by energy cost increases.

Energy policies at the state, federal, and local levels must take into account that incomes will continue to lag behind inflation, an important component of which is energy costs.

In addition, the population is aging. The elderly, many living on fixed incomes, are deeply affected by federal energy policies. That this is more a function of their income than of energy costs per se does not make it any easier to address. The role of energy costs in creating a new class of "low-income" senior citizens must be explored.

THE LOW-INCOME HOUSEHOLDS' BUDGET CRUNCH

Inflation has placed low- and fixed-income households in a budget crunch. The poor have less leeway in their budgets to respond to rising prices for necessities than other income groups. The unexpected and rapid rise in energy costs presented these households with a very dangerous financial dilemma—static resources and dynamic costs.

American life–styles and expectations prior to the 1970s were based on

Table 2.3

Average Annual Expenditures for Selected Categories by Quintiles of Income, 1980–81

Item	Low Income (Lowest 20%)[a]		
	Amount	Percent of Total Expenditures	Rank
Total expenditures	$7,852	100%	
Food	1,820	23.2	1
Shelter	1,526	19.4	2
Fuels[d]	463	5.9	5
Telephone	218	2.7	6
Water and other public services	58	.7	7
Transportation	1,251	15.9	3
Health care	476	6.0	4
Total "necessities"	5,812	74.0	

Item	Moderate Income (Second 20%)[b]		
	Amount	Percent of Total Expenditures	Rank
Total expenditures	$11,570	100%	
Food	2,452	21.2	1
Shelter	2,002	17.3	3
Fuels[d]	636	5.5	4
Telephone	280	2.4	6
Water and other public services	79	.7	7
Transportation	2,278	19.7	2
Health care	595	5.1	5
Total "necessities"	8,322	71.9	

Item	Median Income (Total Complete Reporting)[c]		
	Amount	Percent of Total Expenditures	Rank
Total expenditures	$17,301	100%	
Food	3,201	18.5	2
Shelter	2,797	16.2	3
Fuels[d]	793	4.6	4
Telephone	341	2.0	6
Water and other public services	111	.6	7
Transportation	3,454	20.0	1
Health care	729	4.2	5
Total "necessities"	11,426	66.0	

[a]Income before taxes-$3,473
[b]Income before taxes-$9,791
[c]Income before taxes-$19,989
[d]Includes natural gas, electricity, fuel oil and other fuels.

Source: U.S., Department of Labor, Bureau of Labor Statistics, *Consumer Expenditure Survey: Interview Survey, 1980–1981* (Washington, D.C.: U.S. Government Printing Office, April 1985), p. 11, Table 1.

the assumptions that the price of energy would remain relatively cheap and that the supply would remain uninterrupted. Until 1972 the assumptions seemed reasonable. From 1960 through 1972 the real price of energy declined by 15.8 percent.[9]

In the fall of 1973 these assumptions were dealt a lethal blow. Oil prices skyrocketed, setting off a spiral of higher energy prices from which we have not yet recovered. The energy crisis, as it came to be called, ushered in an era of high energy prices and uncertain supplies.

Between 1972 and 1979, fuel oil prices increased more than 210 percent.[10] Between 1973 and 1977 the income of households with median incomes below the federal poverty level increased by 34.7 percent. During the same period, the Consumer Price Index of household energy fuels increased by 78 percent.[11] The cost of energy is a large factor in the Consumer Price Index, which increases the real differences between energy price increases and nonenergy price increases. As a result, low-income households pay between 22 and 36 percent of their incomes on energy.

In 1984 the National Consumer Law Center studied the impact of energy prices on those receiving Supplemental Security Income (SSI) and Unemployment Compensation. The Center found that households receiving unemployment benefits spent between 11.1 percent (in California) and 49.5 percent (in New Hampshire) of this benefit for home energy. In 32 states, households receiving unemployment benefits were left with less than $100 per week after paying winter energy bills.[12]

The FOMAC estimates that the poor lost over $14 billion in purchasing power between 1978 and 1980 because of increases in energy costs.[13]

After paying for food, rent, work–related expenses, and energy, a typical low-income family with a working head of household and small children in day-care has exceeded its monthly budget. To pay for clothing, health care, and other necessities—not to mention discretionary items—they must cut back spending in the first four mentioned areas.

The way in which energy prices relatively affect low-income households' spending is explained in an analysis by Lester Thurow:

While a 100 percent increase in the price of energy would reduce the real income of the average American by 9.9 percent it would have reduced the real income of the poorest decile of families by 34 percent and the richest decile by 5 percent. The real income effects among the poor are almost seven times as large as they are among the rich.[14]

An important issue with far–reaching implications is Thurow's finding that the top 10 percent of all households would actually *benefit* from higher energy prices, based on his estimation that they (the top 10 percent) own over 90 percent of all corporate stock. If this is true with respect to energy resources, Thurow concludes that

since the income gains to the top 10 percent from owning energy resources would be almost five times as large as their income loss from having to pay higher energy prices, a free market for energy would have resulted in a sharp shift toward inequality in the distribution of income.[15]

In light of these distributional effects of energy prices, the way in which low-income families adjust to rising prices to bring down the cost of heating or cooling their homes becomes very important. A look at the way in which low-income households deal with the problem on their own without government involvement offers clues to appropriate policies.

DO THE POOR USE MORE ENERGY?

As the price of energy and the percentage of income devoted to paying for it rise, how do low-income households adjust their energy consumption habits?

The classical economic short-term response to rising energy prices is to curtail energy consumption, to turn down thermostats, close off rooms, and/or eliminate the use of certain appliances.

The general capacity of low-income households to undertake these measures emerges as a threshold concern. While there again are no definitive data available, a review of other studies and an analysis of relevant data by Bernard J. Freiden found that low-income households are limited from the start by their energy-inefficient homes:

Only 41 percent of the lowest fifth have insulation in their homes and less than a third have storm windows. They drive older cars, manufactured before the new federal mileage requirements took effect, and their aging appliances presumably are less efficient than newer models. Yet they do not use much energy—only a third as much energy as the well-to-do, counting indirect consumption.[16]

If one examines direct consumption alone, poor households are estimated to consume about two-thirds as much energy as average households. Most of this direct consumption is devoted to essentials—space heating, water heating, and cooking.

However, the difficulty of generalizing about low-income energy usage is illustrated by an analysis done by the U.S. Department of Health and Human Services,[17] which found that energy expenditures by LIHEAP recipients tended to be higher than average for residential space heating.

An analysis done by the East Ohio Gas (EOG) Company in Cleveland also seems to contradict the premise that poor families use less energy. An examination of actual annual utility bills of customers receiving some form of assistance—either through the federal LIHEAP program, the Ohio Energy Credits (OEC) Program (which serves the low-income elderly and disabled), or the Percentage of Income Payment Plan (PIPP)—revealed that those customers receiving the highest level of assistance had higher than average yearly bills (see Table 2.4). All residential customers spent an average of $823 per year for gas. Those customers receiving OEC and LIHEAP benefits (a maximum of 70 percent of their winter bill being subsidized), paid an average of $1,084 per year. Only those customers receiving OEC paid less than all customers ($802 per year) and these customers are mostly elderly.

These findings could be attributed to a variety of factors. A methodological explanation for the difference between EOG's findings and other studies that say the poor use less could be that EOG looked only at gas customers who pay for their gas directly. Renters, whose energy costs are included in rent, were not considered. It could also be that those receiving assistance have little incentive to conserve since they know that up to 70 percent of their winter heating bill will be paid regardless of how much they use. However, it could also be that those with the lowest incomes (assistance recipients) have the least control over their energy usage.

The amount of energy used for home heating is directly related to the type, age, and condition of the housing stock. Low-income households tend to occupy into the nation's older housing stock, which is generally less energy-efficient and more dilapidated than newer units. This results in low-income households spending more on these essentials than a comparable family living in more efficient housing.

The low level of energy efficiency in housing occupied by low-income households is once again due in part to the assumption implicit in most housing construction before the energy crisis: that energy supplies would always be cheap and plentiful.[18]

For example, about half of Ohio's occupied housing units were built prior to 1940, before Federal Housing Administration standards required insula-

Table 2.4
Average Bill Comparison[a] LIHEAP/PIPP/OEC

Account Type	Number of Accounts	Average Base Load	Average Degree-Day Factor (MCF/Degree-Day)	Estimated Yearly Bill[b] (In Dollars)
LIHEAP[c]	91,899	3.6	.0191	873
PIPP[d]	47,958	4.1	.0218	989
OEC[e]	61,976	3.1	.0178	802
OEC and HEAP	5,406	4.2	.0246	1,084
All residential customers	932,730	3.6	.0175	823

[a]Based on the April 1985 revenue month

[b]Based on $5.10/MCF and $4.28 monthly service charge; calculated using the degree-day averages of 6,178 degree-days. Formula: $5.10 [(Baseload $\times$ 12) + (DDF $\times$ DD)] + ($4.28 $\times$ 12) = Estimated Yearly Bill.

[c]LIHEAP = Low-Income Home Energy Assistance Recipients

[d]PIPP = Percentage of Income Plan Participants

[e]OEC = Ohio Energy Credits Recipients

Source: East Ohio Gas Company, 1985. Reprinted with permission.

tion. As of 1977, an estimated 50 percent of Ohio's 3 million housing units had no insulation and an additional 25 percent were underinsulated.

Much uninsulated housing has filtered down to low-income families, whose housing choices are constrained by both finances and exclusionary housing patterns. (Filtering down can be defined as the process by which low-income households move into housing units previously occupied by higher income families who vacated in favor of higher quality housing, the housing units the low-income households move from being more likely to be condemned and/or razed.) These constraints implicitly limit the family's choice in the energy consumptive aspects of their housing unit.[19] Some low-income housing is in such bad condition that conservation efforts without a coordinated rehabilitation effort would be futile.

The Department of Energy's Weatherization Assistance Program often wasted funds because of its failure to recognize the need for coordinated rehabilitation. Leaking attics were insulated, but the effectiveness of the insulation was severely limited by the leaks. Windows were caulked and weather stripped; they were replaced soon after. As one observer noted:

Unlike new housing which generally requires modifications or additions to existing insulation, oil burners, window caulking, and other structural features and equipment, older housing stock requires major conversion, overhaul and costly initial energy conserving measures to reduce consumption appreciably.[20]

As the generally energy-conscious middle- and upper-income population chooses to buy more energy-efficient housing rather than improve what they have, the older, less-efficient housing will filter down to those least able to afford the more expensive housing.

The central issue is not whether low-income households use more or less energy than other income groups, for the studies show that some use more and some use less. Rather the central issue related to low-income energy consumption is the *degree of control* the poor have over their personal household energy consumption and how their energy consumption patterns compare with those of other income groups.

Unless significant steps are taken to improve and weatherize the existing housing stock or to make new, energy-efficient housing available to low-income families, the low-income segment of the population, those with the least choice, will be saddled not only with disproportionately high energy costs but also with those higher costs for a longer period. Moreover, they will continue to have very little control over the amount of energy they use.

The degree of control that low-income households have over their energy consumption is further affected by the fact that they are disproportionately (about 55 percent) renters.[21] Rental units tend to have fewer energy-saving devices in place than owner-occupied units and have a longer payback period after the installation of these devices.[22]

It is generally estimated that multifamily dwelling units consume about 40 percent less heat per square foot than single-family units. Still, these units have conservation potential if certain obstacles can be overcome. One commonly cited obstacle to conservation is master-metering, which hides the cost of consumption from the renter. (Master-metering means metering gas and electricity for a building as a whole, rather than for each individual unit.) Four out of ten low-income renters live in apartments that are master-metered. Consequently four out of ten low-income renters receive no price signals related to the amount of energy they use. Even if they did want to conserve, most have little or no control over their heat.

Replacing master-meters with individual meters may give tenants more incentive to conserve and more control over their heat but there may also be a downside. Replacement could result in higher overall utility bills. In some states tenants in master-metered buildings benefit from the lower per unit energy costs realized by large users. Where there is a declining utility block rate structure with conversion to individual meters, tenants move into the highest rate blocks for small users. (For a more detailed discussion of declining block and life-line rates and their impact on low-income persons, see "Lifeline Electric Rates and Alternative Approaches to the Problems of Low-Income Ratepayers," Cleveland State University, Energy Program, July 1980.)

There is a second obstacle to conservation: Renters seldom have a long-term financial commitment to their housing unit and so have virtually no incentive to allocate their scarce resources to costly insulation or a new furnace. Landlords are sometimes reluctant or unable to invest in conservation if they believe they cannot raise rents to cover their investment, even if they pay for the heat.

Rising energy costs are often cited as a contributor to the abandonment of apartment buildings as landlords are faced with high operating costs and low rents. Cooper et al. found a link between rising energy costs and the deterioration of low-income rental housing and a rapid jump in reports of housing abandonment in lower-income neighborhoods between 1973 and 1979.[23] A successful energy policy must include the incentive necessary to make rental housing more energy efficient for the benefit of both the people who live there and the neighborhoods in which they are located. A careful balance must be struck between improving a building's energy efficiency and protecting the rights of the tenants.

Despite the minimal degree of control that low-income households (both owners and renters) have over home energy use, their initial reaction to rising prices was to cut back. In 1973–74, those with incomes under $5,000 per annum (the lowest group) reduced their consumption of heating and transportation below 1972–73 levels, often sacrificing comfort and convenience to save money. Heating consumption was cut by 15 percent, transportation consumption by 21 percent. These cuts were proportional to cuts made by higher income groups but represented greater sacrifices by the poor.[24]

In recent years the number of households substantially investing in the increased energy efficiency of their housing units remained small while the number who sacrificed comfort and convenience to save energy remained large. The poor continued to make disproportionate sacrifices in response to price increases while the well-off absorbed higher prices without making many changes in their own energy use practices.[25]

A study done by the University of Massachusetts/Boston surveyed a sample of 108 elderly people representing a variety of socioeconomic backgrounds in the Boston area. It found that

the general pattern of cost cutting measures was found to be (listed in the order taken): regulating thermostat, dipping into retirement savings, giving up significant possessions (such as a car) or meaningful roles (such as entertaining friends and family), reducing size of dwelling space, and limiting food intake or that of other necessities (such as medications, etc).[26]

Low-income families tend to occupy the nation's most–energy–inefficient housing and they have little discretionary income to invest in capital improvements to make their homes more efficient. Yet, despite this lack of control, these findings indicate that they tend to take often extreme measures to cut back consumption, at the expense of comfort and even safety.

LOW-INCOME HOUSEHOLDS AND CONSERVATION

Although low-income households have little discretionary income to invest in conservation measures, many do make such investments, even without government assistance. Several surveys (the 1979 Annual Housing Survey; DOE's National Interim Energy Conservation Survey [NIECS] 1977, 1978; and Residential Energy Conservation Survey, 1979–80) found that the proportion of households with incomes below $5,000 per annum that invested in conservation was smaller than the corresponding proportion of higher income groups. However, another study found that the near-poor (incomes between $5,000 and $10,000 per annum) invested in insulation at the same rate as people in middle-income brackets.[27] There was no consistent pattern among income groups in terms of making cutbacks (close off rooms, turn down furnace and water heater thermostats, and so on), but in terms of efficiency investments, higher-income groups were slightly more likely to have invested in increased energy efficiency (install a more efficient furnace, insulate attic, insulate walls, and such).

A communitywide survey of household energy use taken in February 1980 in Saint Paul, Minnesota, found similar patterns, as Table 2.5 illustrates.

All the studies agreed that the poor are severely limited in their ability to make future investments in conservation. They require an almost im-

Table 2.5

Percentage of Households Making Lifestyle Sacrifices and Energy Efficiency Investments, Saint Paul, Minnesota, 1980

	Household Income				
	Less than $10,000	$10,000-15,999	$16,000-24,999	$25,000-or more	Total
Lifestyle cutbacks					
Close off rooms	63%	56%	56%	54%	58%
Turn down furnace thermostat	85	87	90	92	89
Turn down water heater thermostat	66	65	70	66	67
Efficiency investments					
Install a more efficient furnace	22	23	26	29	25
Insulate attic	51	50	57	64	56
Insulate walls	40	39	42	47	42

Source: Saint Paul, Minnesota, Energy Office, data of Saint Paul Energy Mobilization Survey, February 1980, in Bernard J. Frieden, *Household Energy Consumption: The Record and the Prospect,* M.I.T. Program on Neighborhood and Regional Change, Cambridge, Massachusetts, 1981. Reprinted with permission.

mediate payback—six months—for an investment of $100, and need a year and a half payback to justify an investment of $500. Obviously the poor have little margin for further cutbacks or substantial conservation investments without some form of financial assistance.[28]

In terms of national energy goals, improving the thermal efficiency of existing residences has been estimated to be the most economical way to reduce the nation's energy costs. Experts proclaim:

If simple insulation packages—such as six-inch ceiling insulation, storm windows and doors, caulking, weatherstripping—were installed in 20 million poorly insulated homes, it has been estimated that energy use in the residential sector could be cut by a quarter.[29]

If it is a national energy policy goal to save energy and become more energy independent, then it should be in the best interest of both the nation and individual consumers to have a well-insulated, energy efficient housing stock.

Yet the cost-effectiveness of low-income energy conservation programs has not been determined. This raises two questions concerning energy policy for the poor. How much emphasis should be placed on low-income energy conservation in an overall national conservation strategy? If energy conservation is seen as a means of reducing low-income households' utility bills, how much can they really expect to save? These two questions are discussed next.

Federal, state and local governments have enacted a variety of conservation incentives, which include price decontrol, grants and low interest loans, tax credits, and, in some states, energy efficiency standards. (At least one state, Minnesota, and several localities, including Portland, Oregon, have energy efficiency standards that apply to all homes at the point of sale. These standards can be designed to encourage energy savings in the residential sector, to limit vulnerability to fossil fuel shortages, and to reduce the impact of rising energy costs on renters.) Since the early 1970s there has been a 20–30 percent decline in household energy consumption nationwide. However, because of lack of income and inaccessible credit markets, and low levels of energy consumption, many households, particularly the poor and elderly, are not moved by these incentives. Urban areas, housing large numbers of the poor and elderly, are effectively ignored by energy incentives.

Low-income households conserve to the maximum extent possible, within their limited means. The capacity of low-income households to conserve is limited by their low income, by the condition of the housing units their incomes allow, and by the condition of the heating systems of their units. If conservation is seen as a desirable "social good," then policies must be developed that either offer real incentives for low-income households to conserve more or increase those households' ability to respond to rising prices by expanding their resources.

It is very important to compute accurately the actual energy savings over the life of any conservation-oriented modifications, particularly for low- and moderate-income people. The estimated payback period has a significant impact on a household's willingness and ability to invest in weatherization. One of the major objections to weatherization projects is their high initial cost in light of uncertain long-term savings—will the new system pay for itself before it wears out?

Although the federal government has had programs since 1973 that weatherize the low-income housing stock, little is known about the effectiveness of the program measures undertaken in terms of conserving energy and reducing the burden of rising energy prices on the poor. Several studies found that actual energy savings for low-income households are lower than had been estimated. This may be owing, in part, to overestimates of the given improvement's energy savings potential.

It may also be a result of the failure to take into account changes in the family's activity patterns. It is possible that before receiving weatherization assistance people turn down thermostats or close off rooms to save money. Once their housing units are insulated, people turn up their thermostats, or open previously unused rooms, potentially increasing the level of comfort without increasing energy consumption or raising their monthly bills. This would result in little, if any, energy conservation.

Studies conducted by the Oak Ridge National Laboratory, the Department of Energy, and the State of Ohio found average energy savings per house of 14, 13.4, and 13 percent, respectively. This is compared with projected savings by the American Society of Heating, Refrigeration and Air Conditioning Engineers (ASHRAE) of 20 percent. The Michigan Public Service Commission studied a small number of homes and found that energy savings from weatherization were only about 60 percent of ASHRAE estimates. As more is learned about the energy savings that can be achieved through different conservation measures, programs are adjusted to give priority to the most cost-effective measures. This is resulting in higher savings.

In addition to being affected by the household's behavior, the consumption capacity of any given dwelling is closely linked to the age, condition, and type of the dwelling. The extent to which low- and moderate-income households occupy homes built prior to the establishment of housing codes that included minimum standards for insulation, together with the condition of that housing, in large part determines their need for weatherization. (Prior to the 1950s FHA had no insulation standards. In the 1950s the standards were 1.5 inches, in the 1960s they were 3 inches, in the 1970s with the oil embargo, they were 6 inches, and they have been raised to 10 inches.)

Both weatherization and rehabilitation contribute to meeting the nation's goal of providing a decent, safe, and sanitary home for every American as stated in the National Housing Act of 1949—and the two programs complement one another. It is more efficient to install energy-conserving devices at the same time other home improvements are being made because of the positive conservation synergy of the two.

Separating the two programs can be counterproductive. A dilapidated house or one with a leaking roof or broken windows cannot be effectively weatherized. Weatherization *with* rehabilitation maximizes each program's impact.

Still more can be done. Cities, through their community development block grants, housing rehabilitation programs, and zoning and housing codes can offer further incentives for low-income households for energy conservation. This is discussed in more detail in Chapter 5.

POLICY IMPLICATIONS

It should be a prime objective of national energy policy to help low- and moderate-income households adjust to and control rising energy prices. We have seen that the poor lack the resources for investment in conservation, demand a very short payback period, and generally do not own the homes in which they live. These characteristics inhibit their ability to undertake energy conservation measures in response to price signals alone. An entirely different policy approach is required.

This understanding and the understanding of how low-income households use energy and how they respond to price increases can help policy makers meet the needs of this group while at the same time serving overall national and state objectives of conservation.

This overview of the direct impact of energy price increases on the poor indicates that broad policies are needed that can address long- and short-term needs, both to conserve energy and to pay bills. These policies must also address the different facets of the problem—its impact on low-income housing choices, and its impact on energy conservation.

Since they cannot control the price, low-income households need the resources to adjust to and control the amount of energy they consume. These needs would best be addressed through a strategy coordinated at the federal, state, and local levels to draw on a regionally tailored combination of program approaches.

3

Energy and Cities

Energy usage and pricing patterns in cities have special significance for energy-assistance policy. Cities house a high proportion of the poor, including those most in need of energy assistance, the elderly poor, and also have a high proportion of older housing units and rental housing units. (The Bureau of the Census 1977 *Annual Housing Survey* states that approximately 82 percent of all rental dwellings are located in urban areas.) Being older, many of these units have inefficient heating systems, lack insulation, and as a result have unmanageable heating bills. These festering problems can create major problems for urban areas—mortgage default, abandonment, and, eventually, the need for demolition.

The most pressing component of the problem of energy and the poor for urban areas is its impact on the urban housing stock. A comparison between the Consumer Price Indexes for all urban consumers for 1972 (pre-energy crisis), 1978 (mid-energy crisis), and 1985 shows that while all housing costs have risen, energy costs have risen at a faster rate than any other components (see Table 3.1).

The Northeast is deeply affected by this problem. It has more multifamily rental stock than other regions. Worse, this stock is old and in most cases totally uninsulated. Utility costs account for about *half* of all operating expenses in this housing.[1] The region's dependence on fuel oil for home heating further exacerbates the problem. Fuel oil is priced higher and its price has risen faster than its two major competitors, natural gas and electricity.

The impact of rising energy prices on low-income households affects their housing situation and the urban areas in which they reside in several important ways. It affects their ability to honor their mortgages, to purchase homes, and to pay rent. It also affects the overall quality and quantity of low-income housing. These effects deserve close examination.

Table 3.1

Inflation of Selected Components of Housing Costs: A Comparison[a]: 1972, 1978, 1985

	Dec. 1972	Dec. 1978	Percent Change 72-78	Dec. 1985	Percent Change 78-85
Housing	131.2[b]	211.2	61.0	356.4	68.8
Shelter	136.7	220.5	61.3	392.4	78.0
Rent	121.0[b]	169.5	40.1	272.4	61.0
Home-ownership[c]	142.4	238.9	67.9	NA	NA
Maintenance and repairs	144.2[b]	234.4	62.6	373.7	59.4
Fuel and other utilities	121.7	219.4	80.3	396.6	80.8
Fuels	NA	252.1	NA	488.2	93.6
Fuel oil, coal and bottled gas	NA	309.3	NA	660.6	113.6
Gas (piped) and electricity	122.4	236.0	92.8	445.1	88.6
Other utilities and public services	120.4[b]	159.8	32.7	245.8	53.8
Household furnishings and operation	122.4	184.0	50.3	249.4	35.5
All items	127.3[b]	202.9[b]	59.4	327.4[b]	61.4

[a]All numbers are seasonally adjusted and are for all urban consumers unless otherwise noted. (In 1972, the Bureau of Labor Statistics did not differentiate between urban consumers and urban workers.)

[b]Not seasonally adjusted.

[c]In October 1981, the Bureau of Labor Statistics changed the treatment of home-ownership costs, effective with release of data for January 1985.

Note: NA = Not Available

Sources: U.S. Department of Labor, Bureau of Labor Statistics, *The Consumer Price Index for December 1972*, April 1973, pp. 13, 24, Tables 2, 8; *The Consumer Price Index for December 1978*, March 1979, p. 10, Table 2; and *The Consumer Price Index for December 1985*, February 1986, p. 11, Table 2.

MORTGAGE DEFAULTS

Rising energy costs have increased the low-income household mortgage default rate. Lenders have a general rule of thumb that no more than 25–30 percent of houshold income be spent on housing because defaults become more frequent if housing demands a greater percentage. Yet energy costs, a virtually uncontrollable and significant housing expense, are not routinely considered in calculating the percentage. Energy price rises push households to spend an increasing proportion of their income on housing, often as much as 20–30 percent of their income on energy alone.

A study by Booz Allen concluded that "rising energy prices have a significant effect on the rate of mortgage defaults among low-income homeowners."[2] The study demonstrated the problem is especially critical for homeowners earning less than $6,750 per annum. Households at or about this income level cannot adjust to unforeseen cost increases, resulting in mortgage default with the rise in energy prices above the historical level.[3]

HOME OWNERSHIP

Rising energy costs also affect the ability of moderate-income households to purchase homes. Most moderate-income households depend upon federally insured mortgages to purchase homes. (The Federal Housing Administration's Sections 203, 205, and 235 of the National Housing Act of 1934, The Farmer's Home Administration's [FHA] 502 program, and the Veteran Administration's [VA] Section 1800 program enabled a few low-income households to purchase homes.) These programs traditionally require lower income standards than lending institutions. The increasing number of defaults and the federal government's desire to reduce its obligations in this area caused the income standards for granting loans or ensuring mortgages to be increased, thus reducing the number of moderate-income households eligible to purchase homes. But the requirement of higher loan-to-income ratios discourages private financing in low-income neighborhoods, making mortgage loans even harder to obtain.

The FHA and FMHA have severely limited mortgage assistance to low-income families. This trend is especially pronounced in new construction. Potential low-income homeowners are forced to look to the existing, less–energy–efficient housing stock with its higher energy costs and an absence of retrofit assistance.

The resultant increased default rate and reductions in the availability of mortgages affect low-income areas of cities as well as the people who would live in those areas. Many central cities already suffer from the effects of disinvestment on the part of lenders. The absence of FHA and VA mortgages, which traditionally supply financing in these areas, can only lead to further disinvestment.

RENTAL HOUSING

Just as rising energy prices increase the cost of home ownership, they also affect the affordability of rental housing. Most low-income renters depend on government subsidies to help pay their rent. The brunt of proposed changes in eligibility requirements for rental subsidy programs and cuts in public housing authorities' operating budgets will fall on low-income renters.

There are estimated to be 3.4 million federally assisted housing units nationwide. Of these, 1.3 million are under public housing authorities. Public housing authorities have experienced rapidly rising maintenance costs largely because of increased utility bills. One solution—utility surcharges—causes vast numbers of tenants to pay more than 30 percent of their income on housing costs. (The National Housing Act requires that families living in federally subsidized housing pay no more than 30 percent of their income on rent. The government pays the rest.) Proposed reductions in public housing operating subsidies combined with further rises in energy costs can only lead to "rapid deterioration of public housing, putting the health and safety of those living there at risk and encouraging urban unrest."[4]

Quite apart from increasing the amount low-income urban renters pay for housing, proposed changes in federal housing policy would affect the level of energy efficiency in housing units available to the poor. A switch from a policy focused on rehabilitation and some new construction to the proposed housing vouchers would eliminate one component of federal energy assistance for the poor—cost–effective energy conservation standards. While not always effective, at least these standards provide minimum levels of various energy efficiency features considered cost–effective in the rehabilitation of low-income housing subsidized by the federal government.

Housing vouchers would eliminate federal government control over the quality (including energy efficiency) of housing units occupied by the poor. While in the abstract the voucher system enables individual households to choose units that best suit their needs, the severe shortage of decent, habitable rental housing would force real-world low-income households into competition for the fewer available low-rent apartments, as well as requiring both winners and losers to spend substantially more for their housing.

In the short run, the lack of adequate incentives for either landlords or tenants to invest in energy–efficiency improvements in rental housing results in higher–than–necessary energy costs or higher rents for low- and moderate-income tenants. In the long run, it leads to deferred maintenance, disinvestment, abandonment, and eventually demolition.

A report on energy conservation in rental housing prepared by the Executive Office of Energy Resources of the Commonwealth of Massachusetts describes two other dimensions of the problem:

As energy prices rise, the incentive to invest in conservation actually decreases, since less capital is available for long-term investments and more is required to maintain short-term operating and maintenance expenses. In addition, tax laws may act as a disincentive for conservation investments since fuel costs can be written off as expenses, whereas savings from conservation investments are considered taxable income.[5]

The Technical Development Corporation (TDC) in Boston developed a model program in an attempt to offer incentives to both tenants and building owners. Unique among attempts to retrofit rental housing the program includes no rent–control provisions or lease revisions. Both discourage building owners' participation. Rather, it is based solely on the self-interests of the parties. The model was first tested in Roxbury, Massachusetts, sponsored by the Citizens Conservation Corporation and the Shawmut Bank of Boston. The program targeted low- and moderate-income tenants and building owners in investor-owned and owner-occupied buildings in target neighborhoods. Like an energy management corporation, the program worked on the principle that investments in energy conservation yield sufficient earnings to both cover their cost and provide additional cash flow benefits to the energy consumer or manager. (In the TDC model, these benefits accrue to the tenants.) The program has been adapted for statewide use by the Massachusetts Housing Finance Agency and is funded through oil overcharge funds.

. The building owner cost is subsidized through a combination of loan guarantees and below-market interest rates made possible through a grant from a guarantor (in this case the Massachusetts Housing Finance Agency (MHFA)—which might be a corporation, a foundation, a public finance agency, a Block Grant fund, or the like—who deposits an amount equal to all or a significant portion of the cost of the program in a participating bank at a reduced interest rate. Part of the grant is used directly to cover organizational expenses.

After the deposit the bank makes a conservation loan to the building owner at a below-market interest rate. The spread between two rates covers the bank's administration costs.

The building owner agrees to make payments equal to the amount that would have been paid on a budget billing plan to the fuel provider in the absence of the conservation improvements, adjusting for price increases and variations in weather. From the building owner's payment, the bank pays the actual monthly fuel bill (after conservation improvements) and deducts the debt service. Any remaining funds are deposited into an escrow account that is drawn upon during the coldest months to mail an allotment to tenants as an incentive to continue their energy-saving behavior. A tenant education program is also included to instruct tenants in ways to maximize their rebates. The benefits accrue to both the building owner and the tenant.

HOUSING ABANDONMENT

Rising energy costs affect the supply of low-income housing. They lead to disinvestment in low-income neighborhoods, deferrred maintenance, and increasing rents, which in turn lead to abandonment and eventually to demolition.

Abandonment is a complex, dynamic process with physical, social, and economic components. The part that rising energy costs play in an owner's decision to abandon a building has not been quantified but appears to be growing. A study of housing abandonment done by the U.S. Comptroller General surveyed residents in 149 cities. The respondents perceived the following causes of abandonment to be the most serious: (1) physical deterioration of buildings, (2) absentee ownership by landlords, and (3) increasing cost of home operation and maintenance.

Energy costs are a significant part of operating and maintenance costs. In the decade from 1969 to 1979, energy costs accounted for about 40 percent of the total increase in operating costs for rental housing.[6] Any sudden rise could therefore trigger abandonment. It is no coincidence that the shut-off of utilities is so often the final step in making a building uninhabitable. A Jersey City, New Jersey, housing official pointed out:

Taxes and energy are the keys to abandonment in this city. What happens is that increased taxes and rising energy costs come at the same time that these older buildings are due for major repairs. But landlords cannot jack the rents up because people are too poor. The smaller landlords are usually well in over their heads already and they do not know how to cope. They sell to the large absentee owners who cut services and the good tenants move out.[7]

The extent to which rising energy costs lead to abandonment needs further study and analysis. The connection should be of major concern to cities trying to deal with the problems of abandonment and supply of housing for low-income households.

The energy crisis has created special problems for our urban areas. Residents tend to look to their local government to find solutions to their own energy–related problems, yet cities have been affected, too. High concentrations of low-income families, substandard housing, and rental housing coupled with rising energy prices have contributed to mortgage defaults, deterioration, and abandonment. Further, those cities in the high–energy–consuming states have witnessed a loss of business and industry and tax dollars to the sunbelt states, leaving them less able to cope with their own energy–related problems.

Most cities have established energy offices to at least deal with wasteful energy consumption within city government. Some have developed more broad-based programs in attempts to stem the increase in abandonment and the loss of industry and to protect their tax base.

The more information we gain about the energy assistance problem, the larger it seems. It touches all aspects of the low-income person's life. It is a welfare problem in that it is a function of household income and it affects the budget and spending capacity of the low-income household; it is a housing problem in that it is a function of the quality of housing and it affects the household's capacity to rent, to purchase, or to maintain their homes; it is an energy problem in that it is a function of rising energy prices and in that it affects a household's capacity to conserve; and it is an urban problem in that as low-income households tend to be concentrated in urban areas, their inability to deal with rising energy prices creates problems for cities— abandonment, demolition, and a general shortage of adequate low-income housing.

However, the breadth of the problem is not reflected in the policies and programs designed to address it. Part II will discuss the development of these policies and programs, their strengths and their shortcomings, and options for effectively dealing with the low-income energy problem.

PART II

THE PUBLIC SECTOR RESPONSE

4

The Case For Federal Intervention

The important role that energy plays in the U.S. economy and in national defense has made its production and distribution a major policy concern of federal and state governments for at least the past 50 years. The rising energy prices of the past decade added a new dimension to government energy policy. Policies were adopted that attempted to control prices and, later, to mitigate the impact of rising prices on low-income consumers.

It is important to review the rationale behind federal, state, and local government intervention in energy policy for the poor as well as to describe the evolution and relationship of programs developed at all three levels of government to deal with this problem.

An overview of recent U.S. energy policy, beginning with the Nixon administration, provides the context in which government policies for energy and the poor can be understood. The Nixon administration's response to rising energy prices was to expand and extend the expiring economywide price controls on petroleum. Late in 1973, Congress enacted the Emergency Petroleum Allocation Act, which established a comprehensive system of price and allocation controls throughout domestic crude oil production, refining, and marketing. In addition, a system of entitlement benefits was established to distribute the costs of imported oil across all industry firms, along with mandatory and voluntary measures to encourage conservation. These controls have since been removed in favor of a more efficiency-oriented policy approach.[1]

Cox and Wright contend that

these policies were obviously undertaken because the shock of the oil price increases raised serious questions about the financial burdens that higher energy costs and inflation would place on certain consuming groups. There was a widespread belief that the federal government had the responsibility for ensuring that these burdens were shared equitably among all consuming and producing sectors.[2]

The development of price controls suggests a clearly focused, albeit ill-conceived, policy approach, based on the premise that energy must be priced and allocated by the federal government "fairly and equitably" among consumers. The subsequent lifting of these controls created an unfair and inequitable burden for low-income consumers.

The energy crisis of the 1970s raised the nation's consciousness about energy and its impact on the poor, making this aspect of energy policy politically visible. Many strong interest groups representing consumers, utilities, welfare, and housing officials lobbied for, and won, programs to help the poor.

Yet the role of government in protecting low-income households from rising energy costs has never been clearly defined in legislation, even though the need for protection was articulated by the Carter administration in the first National Energy Plan. The debate over the role of federal government in this dimension of energy policy has raged since the mid 1970s and incorporates several arguments:

1. The lifting of government control of energy prices and production contributed to the rapid rise in prices and created an expectation for continued government intervention in the area of energy. Energy assistance was seen as a means of protecting the poor from the effects of these policies.

2. Energy is a necessity or "merit good," a minimum or life-sustaining amount of which must be guaranteed, regardless of income. The government must be the guarantor.

3. Energy is an important component in many other government-sponsored programs—that is, housing, welfare, utility rate reform, economic development, and community development. These programs fall well within the public interest, therefore energy falls within the public interest.

THE EMERGENCE OF FEDERAL PROGRAMS

Energy assistance programs emerged out of the crisis situation created by rapidly rising energy prices in the winter of 1973–74. It became evident that existing income maintenance programs were not keeping up with inflation, let alone escalating energy costs. Households that depended on Social Security, unemployment insurance, AFDC, and SSI, as well as other households "on the edge," were very often devastated by the rapid rise in prices.

The first organized effort by the federal government to deal with this problem was undertaken by the Community Services Administration (CSA, formerly the Office of Economic Opportunity, OEO) on an ad hoc, locally initiated basis, through CSA's local Community Action Agencies (CAAs). In

1974, OEOs director authorized the expenditure by CAAs of up to 10 percent of their general operating funds for energy-related activities, including weatherization and crisis assistance. The former provided insulation, weather stripping, caulking, and other energy conservation measures. The latter provided financial assistance to pay utility bills, or purchase fuel, blankets, or clothing.

In 1975 the Emergency Energy Conservation Program (EECP) was created by the Community Services Act to "enable low-income individuals and families, including the elderly and the near poor, to participate in energy conservation programs designed to lessen the impact of the high cost of energy . . . "[3]

CSA funding for EECP was minimal. However, the severe 1976-77 winter prompted Congress to authorize $200 million for crisis intervention. This marked a turning point in energy assistance. The energy-related problems of the poor began to emerge as a major policy concern. Weatherization and direct assistance branched off and became two separate programs, administered by two separate agencies, with two different funding appropriations.

Direct Assistance

What followed was a series of hastily assembled crisis assistance programs with limited funding, unclear direction, and a constantly changing administrative structure at the federal, state, and local levels. Each program was authorized under the Economic Opportunity Act of 1964, as amended. For each program year, Congress appropriated $200 million. Although the primary purpose of the first three programs was to alleviate crisis situations for low-income persons, the programs varied substantially in their design, implementation, and administration. Administered by CSA, the first three programs to be funded were:

1. *Special Crisis Intervention Program (SCIP), 1977.* SCIP paid up to $250 to utility companies and fuel dealers for needy households. If the household was experiencing hardship, the payment could be used for unpaid bills or for future service. Priority was given for households headed by a person 65 years of age or older.

2. *Emergency Energy Assistance Program (EEAP), 1978.* EEAP allowed up to a $250 payment to utility companies and fuel dealers for needy households. However, it also allowed for other forms of assistance such as blankets, food, medical services, clothing, and space heaters. EEAP disallowed payments for future service.

3. *Crisis Intervention Program (CIP), 1979.* CIP differed considerably from its two predecessors. It contained three separate subprograms: crisis intervention, winter-related disaster relief, and supplemental crisis intervention.

In a pattern that was to characterize the timing of all the crisis assistance programs, 1976–77 SCIP funds were appropriated on May 4, 1977, and grants were not available to the states until July, well after the winter heating crisis had passed. SCIP provided block grants to states that developed approved state plans. The grants were allocated to one designated agency in each state—usually either the state welfare agency or the state economic opportunity agency. The state agency then passed funds on to local agencies to administer.

Like SCIP, EEAP funds were not appropriated until March 7, 1978. By May 20, the scheduled closing date of the program, one-fourth of the funds were still unspent. However, in response to a court order, CSA reopened applications from November of the next fiscal year to the following May, thereby overlapping EEAP with the FY 1979 program. Over the two-year period, $189 million of EEAP funds were distributed to over 865,000 households.

EEAP funds went directly to local CAAs, rather than as block grants to states. The money could only be used on a contingency basis, upon declaration by the director of CSA that certain states or localities had experienced energy- or weather-related emergencies.

CIP was very similar to the FY 1978 EEAP program. Funds were appropriated in October 1978, much earlier than the previous two programs, but, in keeping with tradition, regulations were not issued until the end of January 1979 and funds did not reach many localities until March.

1979 represented a second and more significant turning point in crisis-assistance programs. The energy crisis had escalated as a result of two unrelated actions: (1) In April President Carter announced that he intended to decontrol domestic crude oil prices by October 1, 1981; and (2) OPEC decided to increase the price of crude oil dramatically.

To offset the anticipated increases in prices, the appropriation for energy assistance was increased eightfold to $1.6 billion. The Energy Crisis Assistance Program (ECAP) was signed into law on November 27, 1979, after months of congressional debate and discussion. It had many features of the past crisis assistance programs, but moved closer to an income transfer program in that dollars could automatically go to those who were categorically eligible for other assistance—that is, SSI and AFDC recipients.

Of the total $1.6 billion appropriated through ECAP, $400 million went to CSA for emergency assistance and $1.2 billion was transferred to the Department of Health, Education and Welfare (HEW) (now the Department of Health and Human Services). Of the $1.2 billion, $400 million was earmarked for a special one-time cash payment to SSI recipients and the remaining $800 million, plus any unused SSI funds, was available to states for either cash payments to AFDC recipients or for distribution according to a block grant requiring HEW approval.

ECAP, administered by CSA, was a crisis program, designed to meet life-

or health-threatening energy-related emergencies. The other part of the program, administered by HEW, was designed to help low-income persons cope with rising energy costs caused by recent OPEC price increases and the additional burdens expected to result from crude oil decontrol. Thus it was more of an energy assistance or income maintenance program. However, states that chose the block grant approach were given the choice of using all their funds as crisis assistance, or, conversely, using all their funds as an income maintenance supplement. It left a great deal of discretion to the states in using these funds.

Operational problems plagued all these programs at the state level. The programs presented unusual administrative challenges, particularly in the first year for SCIP. Eligibility and payment systems had to be established. Funds had to be distributed to large numbers of eligible households in a very short time by state and local agencies with little prior experience in this area.

Ohio's experience in administering these programs is illustrative of the problems encountered by other states. Specific problems that Ohio encountered were: (1) lack of administrative funds resulting in a diversion of resources, (2) underspending in the first year owing to the program's late start, (3) lack of lead time to gear up the program, (4) outreach, (5) determination and verification of eligibility, and (6) timing of payments.

Congress took a major step and institutionalized the concept of energy assistance when it passed the Omnibus Budget Reconciliation Act of 1981, Public Law 97–35. Title XXVI of this Act authorized the Low-Income Home Energy Assistance Program in 1980–81. By this time, the federal government had better guidelines for developing its program. For example, the Fuel Oil Marketing Advisory Committee of the Department of Energy studied low-income energy assistance programs and recommended that no American family should pay more than 10 percent of its income for fuel. However, these guidelines were never adopted.

LIHEAP differed significantly from its predecessors because although funds could be used for crisis intervention, it was designed as a broad-based income-transfer program to assist low-income households to meet the costs of home energy. Funds could be used for heating assistance, cooling assistance, crisis assistance, and weatherization. The program was hailed by state program administrators as a long-awaited and much-needed improvement, providing continuity in funding and requirements to a program characterized by confusion and uncertainty. However, this optimism was short-lived. From the outset LIHEAP created numerous administrative problems for the states. The program got a late start, funding levels were uncertain, and regulations left states a great deal of discretion for such things as establishing eligibility and payment systems, verification, applications, payments to building operators, supplemental payments, and two-party checks for the bulk fuel dealers.

1981–82 was the *first* year the program received a long-term three-year authorization. Theoretically, this allowed states to do long-range planning. As one of Reagan's new block grants, it also included several other features that differed from previous programs:

1. 15 percent program funds could be used for weatherization activities.
2. 10 percent of program funds could be transferred to another block grant.
3. Eligibility was raised from 125 to 150 percent of the poverty guidelines.
4. Checks for bulk fuel, master-metered, and nonparticipating utilities were made directly to the recipient.
5. An emergency set-aside fund, 100 percent application process, central processing, and verification were included.

Weatherization proponents in many states have succeeded in convincing state legislatures to set aside the allowable 15 percent of LIHEAP funds for weatherization. This is, in part, an attempt to offset the uncertainties of federal weatherization funding. Most states have transferred a portion of LIHEAP funds to other block grants. (In FY 1983, 30 states transferred a total of approximately $115 million in LIHEAP funds to other block grants, according to a study done by the U.S. Department of Health and Human Services, Social Security Administration, Office of Family Assistance, Office of Energy Assistance, entitled "Low-Income Home Energy Assistance Program, Report to Congress for Fiscal Year 1983.")

Other federal programs that provide direct assistance to low-income households in case of energy emergencies are the AFDC and General Relief emergency payments. These are one-time payments available to offset any emergency, including those that are energy-related.

Much of the initial confusion surrounding direct assistance programs seems to have diminished as a result of the three-year appropriation and the fact that state administrators are becoming more familiar with the programs. Yet, despite the increases in federal funding, program funding is still inadequate to meet the needs. In FY 1983, in an attempt to offset this, states used almost $23 million of a $200 million petroleum violation escrow fund to supplement LIHEAP. (Under PL 97–377, Section 155, $200 million in "Oil Overchange Funds" was made available to the state for use under LIHEAP or any of four energy conservation programs administered by the Department of Energy.)

Weatherization

While the weatherization component of energy assistance has a less confused past than direct assistance, it also has a more uncertain future.

The need for weatherization assistance is acute. The federal government's reliance on price signals to spur conservation places the low-income households in a trap. They cannot afford *not* to weatherize their homes, but without government assistance they cannot afford to weatherize. They are dependent upon direct assistance programs to meet immediate needs—paying utility bills—but they have no way to reduce those bills over the long run.

Federal weatherization assistance programs, like direct assistance programs, grew out of the original CSA crisis assistance demonstration projects. The success and popularity of these early projects, coupled with a growing need, convinced Congress of the need for a weatherization program on a national level. However, the weatherization programs were hampered by constantly changing regulations, procedures, and funding levels.

Weatherization is seen as a means of conserving energy and thereby controlling home energy expenditures. The responsibility for low-income home weatherization was assigned to the Federal Energy Administration (FEA, now the Department of Energy) as part of the Energy Conservation and Production Act of 1976. Low-income weatherization was one small part of the overall goal of making 90 percent of existing U.S. homes more energy efficient. In addition to the FEA program, CSA continued to run its weatherization program.

The two programs were very different in spirit and in practice. They had different eligibility requirements and administrative structures. The only thing both had in common was that they were administered locally by CAAs and they were supposed to weatherize low-income housing. The CSA program proved to be more successful at meeting this goal. CSA's program bypassed the states, giving funds directly to local CAAs to administer. The FEA program required state involvement in the allocation of funds to local policy advisory councils. CSA provided that up to 10 percent of administrative funds could be spent on direct labor and project supervision, while the FEA program relied on Comprehensive Employment and Training Act (CETA) workers. The CSA program required compliance with only very general guidelines, while the FEA program had very specific requirements and standards.

Although logic and efficiency may have dictated combining the two programs, two powerful stakeholder groups succeeded in maintaining the two separate programs at least for a short time. Continuation of the CSA program can be directly attributed to efforts to preserve the Office of Economic Opportunity (now CSA) in the face of the Nixon administration's attempt to dismantle it by assigning one of its largest programs to the FEA. Congress's insistence on maintaining the CSA program succeeded in keeping CSA and the CAAs alive. Even after the program was administered entirely by DOE at the federal level, it continued to be administered locally by the CAAs. As late as 1985, the existence of the CAAs depended in large part on income derived from administration of the weatherization and direct assistance programs.

The level of funding for low-income weatherization increased significantly in 1976 ($200 million was allocated over two years, an amount equal to that for direct assistance). However, homes were not weatherized because of (1) restrictive DOE regulations, (2) state–level administrative problems associated with the new responsibilities of the expanded program, (3) shortages of labor, (4) lack of information transfer and training, (5) problems with rental units, and (6) funding delays by DOE and states.[4]

1977 was a year of much debate about the future of low-income weatherization programs. Hearings on this issue represented the first time that concrete but still sketchy figures were available to Congress on the severity of the impact of rising energy prices on the poor. Several of the studies discussed in Chapter 2 were used as testimony in these hearings. In response to problems realized in the first year of program operation, DOE proposed major changes in program regulations that were incorporated in the National Energy Conservation and Policy Act of 1978 (NECPA). NECPA unified the CSA and the FEA (now DOE) programs together with a third weatherization program run through the Farmers Home Administration (FMHA). (FMHA's weatherization program was limited to loans at 8 percent interest to rural homeowners. NECPA added grants to this program on the same terms as the CSA and DOE programs, except that FMHA provided extra funds for labor.) NECPA raised the total per unit cost ceiling from $400 to $800, standardized DOE and CSA eligibility criteria and material purchase requirements, and authorized expenditures for limited repair materials.

Specifically, all the programs depended largely on workers supported by CETA and so required state dollars to supplement the labor costs of the program. Grants were available to households with income not exceeding 125 percent of the poverty level. Up to $800 could be spent on materials, including furnace efficiency modification, clock thermostats, water heater insulation, multiglazed windows and doors, and heat-reflective window and door material. This $800 also covered the more traditional insulation and caulking and weather stripping materials as well as tools and equipment, transportation, personnel, and incidental repairs. However, other home repairs like patching roofs, replacing doors and windows, and repairing walls were excluded, even though they could have contributed greatly to a home's energy efficiency.

Despite continuous problems with program administration and labor production, the number of homes weatherized slowly began to increase. The program regulations were amended in 1980 to improve the program. These changes included an authorization of up to $600 in funds for labor. Congress raised the maximum allowable expenditure from $800 to $1,000 per unit, thus raising the total amount of the grant per unit from $800 to $1,600, where severe shortages of labor could be documented. It authorized the use of program funds for no-cost/low-cost energy conservation measures as an interim approach to weatherization, and, most important, allowed for the weatherization of multifamily rental units if 66 percent of the occupants were income-eligible. It authorized an appropriation of $200 million for FY 1981.

According to DOE's, *The Weatherization Assistance Program Annual Report* for 1980, these amendments resulted in marked increases in production, from 18,099 homes in January to 28,473 homes in August of 1980, compared with 9,300 and 12,300 homes in the same two periods of 1979.[5] By late 1979 it was estimated that about 1.5 million barrels of oil a year had been saved by the poor. Despite these seeming improvements, the federal government's commitment to energy conservation in general and to conservation for the poor, in particular, has consistently been weak. Threats to terminate the program emerge each year as the appropriations process begins. Appropriated funds for the program ranged from a low of $120 million in 1978 to a high of $245 million in 1983. Congress appropriated only $190 million for weatherization for 1984.

In contrast, LIHEAP was funded at $1.875 billion and received a $200 million supplemental appropriation bringing the total to $2.075 billion for 1984. An additional $18 million was appropriated from petroleum overcharge repayments to DOE, which Congress had earmarked in 1983 for weatherization of homes of the elderly and low-income, and assistance for those who can't pay their heating bills. The Omnibus Budget Reconciliation Act of 1981 permitted states to set aside up to 15 percent of LIHEAP block grant funds for low-income weatherization programs. In 1984, 46 states transferred $201.5 million (more than the total weatherization program appropriation) for this purpose. In most states, these funds have been used to supplement the DOE funds. (See Table 4.1 for a comparison of funding levels between the two programs.)

This transfer of funds at the state level illustrates that while the federal

Table 4.1
U.S. Weatherization Funding and Direct Assistance Funding

U.S. Weatherization Funding (Home Weatherization Grants), FY75-FY84 ($ Billions)

	FY75	FY76	FY77	FY78	FY79	FY80	FY81	FY82	FY83	FY84	FY85	Total
CSA	.02	.03	.08	.06								.19
DOE			.03	.06	.20	.20	.18	.14	.25	.19	.19	1.44
LIHEAP transfer								.14	.20	.19	.23	.76
Total	.02	.03	.11	.12	.20	.20	.18	.28	.45	.38	.42	2.39

U.S. Direct Assistance Funding, FY75-FY84 ($ Billions)

	FY75	FY76	FY77	FY78	FY79	FY80	FY81	FY82	FY83	FY84	FY85	Total
CSA		.20	.20	.20	.20	.40						1.20
HHS						1.20	1.85	1.88	1.98	2.08	2.1	11.09
Oil overcharge funds										.02		.02
Total		.20	.20	.20	.20	1.60	1.85	1.88	1.98	2.10	2.1	12.31

Source: Compiled from information supplied by the U.S. Department of Energy and Department of Health and Human Services.

government is attempting to back out of its responsibility to fund weather-ization, the states continue to value it as a much-needed program. Congress and the administration are apparently not concerned with a long-term approach to keeping fuel bills under control and conserving our energy supplies for future generations.

In fact, since 1979 the federal government's approach to dealing with the problem of energy and the poor has been focused heavily on direct assistance, which is increasingly taking the form of direct payments to utility companies. Conservation for the poor seems to have been determined to be an inappropriate role for the federal government. Rather than developing a coordinated strategy, the federal government has created two very separate programs, run by two separate departments, and placed them in the position of competing for the same pots of money.

While it is difficult to detect any rationale underlying the federal government's shift from a policy focusing equally on direct assistance and conservation, to one that focuses almost exclusively on direct assistance, several factors may explain this shift:

1. The weatherization program was plagued by a variety of problems ranging from funding uncertainties and jurisdictional overlap to labor and equipment problems.

2. The few, preliminary studies that attempted to measure energy savings found that less energy is saved than was originally estimated. This led to the perception that the capacity for energy conservation among low-income households is low, regardless of the level of conservation materials supplied.

3. Differences in consumption patterns, energy prices, housing stock, and so on, led to the conclusion that energy conservation is more appropriately handled (that is, funded) at the state and local levels.

4. The efforts of conservation advocates were spread across a broad range of programs from the promotion of renewable energy sources to load management and conservation pricing of utilities. Low-income programs were only one part of their overall agenda.

5. Home weatherization programs have been the mainstay of the CAAs, agencies that many are trying to phase out. Elimination of the weatherization program—as the Reagan administration proposed—could effectively eliminate many of the CAAs.

Other federally funded programs to improve the energy efficiency of low-income housing include the Department of Housing and Urban Development's cost-effective energy conservation standards for rehabilitation and new construction, the Solar and Conservation Bank, Conservation and Renewable Resources Tax Credits, and the Residential Conservation Service Program.

Department of Housing and Urban Development

The Department of Housing and Urban Development (HUD) encourages energy conservation in its housing programs. Housing rehabilitation financed through the Community Development Block Grant (CDBG) can include measures to increase the energy efficiency of buildings through installation of storm windows and doors; siding, wall, and attic insulation and conversion; modification or replacment of heating and cooling equipment; including solar equipment; and such. Under the Urban Development Action Grant Program, HUD will give more weight to proposals that include some energy conservation measures.

On July 27, 1979, HUD imposed Cost-Effective Energy Standards to encourage the use of energy-efficient techniques/materials for residential renovation in projects funded through rehabilitation programs and in new construction programs.

Public housing offers an opportunity for the government, which acts as both owner and renter to invest in and benefit from conservation. Public housing is notoriously energy inefficient and its conservation capacity is large. Prior to 1973, HUD's minimum property standards could be met with walls of cellophane wrap.

HUD also administers the Solar Energy and Energy Conservation Bank, which subsidizes the cost of borrowing or provides grants to implement solar energy and energy conservation measures. The Bank was authorized in Title V of the Energy Security Act of 1980. However, political infighting left it without an appropriation. After a three-year delay, an initial $50 million appropriation enabled the bank to "open for business" in 1983. By January 1985 the Bank had awarded $65.7 million to 36 states. The Bank's funds are used to support grant and loan programs run by state agencies or local entitlement communities for residential energy conservation.

Less than 13 percent of these Bank funds allocated were used for solar loans. The remainder were used for conservation loans. Of the solar subsidies almost none went to low-income households. On the other hand, 96 percent of the energy conservation loan recipients were low- or moderate-income.

States can use Bank funds to support existing state programs or create new programs to meet their individual residential conservation needs, within specified guidelines and criteria. This program offers states the flexibility to design their own programs but it is limited by its small appropriation and uncertain funding.

Energy Tax Credits

Consistent with its reliance on price to trigger conservation, the major residential conservation thrust of the federal government has been through tax credits. Approximately 3 million taxpayers take about $305 million in credits per year. However, very few of those claiming credits are low-income households.

The Energy Tax Act of 1978 authorized residential energy tax credits for investments in conservation and renewable energy resources in existing principal residences. Many states also offer conservation tax incentives. Credits may be taken for a certain portion of expenditures made between April 20, 1977, and December 31, 1985, for two measures: (1) insulation and other energy conservation components, and (2) equipment to enable the use of nontraditional or renewable energy sources.

The tax credits have performed poorly across all income groups, particularly the low-income. In the first 20 months of availability, only 5.9 million households or 6.5 percent of total tax returns filed claimed the credit. The average value of the expenditure claimed was estimated at $742. However, for low-income households, whose incomes were less than $10,000 and filed returns, only about 1 percent took the credits. On the average, these households spent $665 and received a tax credit of $100.[6]

Steven Ferry of the National Consumer Law Center analyzed tax credits and concluded that not only do low-income households not benefit from the tax credits but the credits are regressive.[7] There are many barriers that prevent low-income households from taking advantage of the tax credits. First and most obvious is their income. Households with little or no tax liability have no tax against which to take a credit. (A tax rebate program offered by several states, on the other hand, offers an incentive even to those who pay no or small amounts of taxes.) A second barrier is the minimum credit of $10.00, which necessitates an expenditure of at least $67.00 in a year on conservation materials. A third barrier excludes low-income renters and absentee landlords from participation, thus excluding a large segment of the rental housing stock. A fourth barrier is the time lag—the benefits of a federal tax credit are not realized until 4 to 16 months after an expenditure is made.

One consultant to HUD calculated that 78 percent of American taxpayers and 65 percent of all present homeowners would be unable to take the full $4,000 solar tax credit because they would not have enough income to offset it.[8] A study by Alan and Ron Okagaki concludes that a low income household is only one sixth as likely as any other income group to benefit from solar tax credits.[9]

Residential Conservation Service

The Residential Conservation Service (RCS) program was implemented in 1979, pursuant to Part I of Title II of the National Energy Conservation Policy Act. It requires states to develop plans through which utilities with annual sales in excess of 10 billion cubic feet of natural gas or 750 million kilowatt hours of electricity will provide energy conservation services to their residential customers. Specifically, utilities must: (1) offer energy audits, upon request; (2) provide information concerning savings in energy costs from energy conservation practices; and (3) arrange for the purchase, installation, financing, and billing of energy conservation and renewable measures, upon request.

Most state plans required a small fee for the energy audit (in Ohio it was $15.00). However, even this small fee precludes many low-income households from participating unless some arrangement can be made to have the fee waived for those households. Regardless of income, few people have taken advantage of the program nationwide. As of April 1983, 40 states had programs in operation. Over 2 million audits had been performed. However, since RCS provides no financial incentive to undertake the conservation measures, it is not clear how many homes were weatherized as a result. (A more detailed discussion of RCS can be found in Chapter 7.)

Rates

A third major policy approach of the federal government in dealing with the problem of energy and the poor was rate reform. The Public Utility Regulatory Policy Act of 1978 (PURPA) encourages the conservation of gas and electricity and the development of equitable rate structures.

Section 114(b) requires state regulatory authorities to consider, and adopt if appropriate, *electric* lifeline rates for low-income households. Lifeline is a price mechanism for alleviating the special hardships of low-income households owing to escalating energy prices, and promoting energy conservation. To address the first objective, the utility bills of low-income households are reduced to a level where "essential energy needs" can be met within the household's limited budget.

To address the second objective, rates are designed to provide a price signal to modify energy use patterns, that is, lower rates in the first rate block and higher rates in the tail blocks. If one makes the assumption that low-income households generally use smaller amounts of electricity and limit their monthly consumption so as not to exceed the first block, conservation rate breaks or inverted rates are compatible with alleviating the special problems of low-income individuals. However since low-income customers often consume more energy than others (see Chapter 2) the conservation and low-income assistance objectives are not necessarily compatible.

Rate structure experiments have taken many forms since the passage of PURPA. They range from rate freezes to so-called lifeline rates, but all are intended to provide some level of discount or benefit to all or a portion of the residential class of ratepayers.

In July 1980 the College of Urban Affairs' Energy Program at Cleveland State University (CSU) completed a series of case studies for the U.S. Department of Energy entitled *Lifeline Electric Rates and Alternative Approaches to the Problems of Low-Income Ratepayers.* The report documented a total of 20 rate programs, 10 of which were considered but not implemented and 10 of which were implemented. CSU has also conducted three 50-state surveys that documented energy assistance programs including special rate structures. The original survey was released in 1979, an update was done in early fall of 1981, and a second update was completed in spring 1985. In addition to documenting the existence of various types of assistance programs, the surveys point to trends in rate reform.

Approximately one-half of the 50 states experimented with and implemented some form of lifeline rates in response to PURPA. The 1979 survey found 23 states had implemented or considered 36 separate rate schedules that provided some level of reduction or discount. By 1981, only 15 special rates were offered in 13 states. Three years later, the number of states offering lifeline rates dwindled to a handful. Only Massachusetts, West Virginia, and New Hampshire have lifeline rates that appear to save customers over $100 per year.

The decline in the number of states offering rate relief to low-income customers can be attributed to two serious issues: equity and administrative efficiency. As states experimented with rate-oriented solutions, they discovered many problems that could not be satisfactorily resolved and turned to other types of programs that were more equitable and easier to administer.

The largest barrier to the implementation of lifeline rates was the issue of equity. Revenue recovery is essential consideration in any rate break. If a portion of a utility company's customers pays less than it would under "normal" circumstances, the lost revenue must be recovered from another source. In almost all instances, this burden fell to ratepayers outside of the target population. As might be expected, this was often the most highly contested issue in rate reduction considerations.

The most formidable opponents of income-related rate reductions are often commercial and industrial ratepayers who do not, for the most part, favor rate subsidies for residential customers at their expense. The implementation of California's Lifeline Act is a good example. During the consideration process, claims were made that lifeline rates were discriminatory, that rates were based on income, not cost of providing service, and that industry would be discouraged from settling in California because of excessive energy costs as a result of the revenue recovery mechanism. The controversial Lifeline Act was adopted in 1975 but was replaced in 1982 by the "Share Bill," which is an inverted rate structure with a conservation incentive. Revenue shortfalls are recovered by residential sales in the second or third blocks.

A rate reduction program that was not as highly contested on this issue was the Maine Demonstration Program. In this instance, nonbenefiting customers were assessed an average of 10 cents a month. A majority of those who complained were just above the eligibility limits and objected to forced subsidization.

Some attempts have been made to circumvent, or at least mitigate, the controversial issue of revenue recovery. In those instances, it was proposed that state general revenues or tax credits for utility companies be used. While this offers a more equitable solution, only West Virginia has chosen this route.

Revenue recovery through rates constitutes a hidden tax on all other ratepayers to support those who cannot pay. Not only is it a hidden tax, but it is a regressive tax in that it raises the price of a basic necessity—energy. The lowest income people, who often use the most energy owing to the inefficiency of their homes, and who pay the largest percentage of their income for energy of any income group, are the ones hardest hit by any rate increase. Those who do not qualify for the special rates are disproportionately penalized by this type of policy.

Determining benefit levels and defining the eligible population also raise equity issues. Obviously, the higher the benefit levels and the number of intended beneficiaries, the higher the amount of revenue that needs to be recovered. But the issue of benefit levels also involves the question of whether beneficiaries should realize a discount regardless of consumption. Most rate programs provide a reduction for only the first block or two of consumption to encourage conservation. After that, rates either reach parity with regular residential rates or increase significantly if an inverted rate schedule is used. (In an inverted rate profile, rates for consumption in excess of the lifeline level [discounted block] are higher than regular rates.) This encourages conservation but also allows for the possibility of revenue recovery from a portion of the target population—those who use more than the lifeline level.

The question in defining the eligible population is, Does anyone other than the intended target population benefit? A tangential premise to this question has often been that low-income households also are low users of energy. Results of studies regarding this theory have been mixed, at best. This may be one explanation for the creation of conservation incentives. No determination beyond consumption level needs to be made.

In the 1981 survey update, 5 of the 14 states covered had a conservation rate. By 1984 13 states had adopted them. Conservation or small use rates are more easily administered and avoid many of the equity issues associated with lifeline rates that are tied to usage.

Most state regulatory commissions are prohibited by law or state constitution from favoring one class or type of customer over another or from discriminating within a customer class. Court decisions have struck down commission orders to implement lifeline rates in many states. Without changes in state laws, it is unlikely that the federal government's push for lifeline rates will have an impact on energy assistance programs in the future.

THE FUTURE OF FEDERAL PROGRAMS

Despite the proliferation of conservation-related programs, the federal government has focused its efforts and its funds for low-income energy assistance in the area of direct assistance rather than conservation.

The federal government's response to the call for energy assistance is similar to its response to many of our social problems. It has taken a politically acceptable, band-aid approach to the problem. Energy assistance began with a community-oriented, crisis-management approach that was successfully initiated by several local CAAs. At that level, money was spent according to specific community needs. Blankets, fuel oil, clothing, payments to fuel providers, and weatherization were all available. The little federal money that was available was subject only to CSA's antipoverty guidelines.

Community needs soon outgrew the small-scale nature of the program. As energy prices continued to rise, more and more money was needed to offset the impact on the poor. The original CAA concept quickly grew into an often unmanageable quagmire of programs with at least four federal agencies issuing volumes of rules, regulations, conditions, and requirements.

In 1979 federal policies advocating price decontrol were linked with massive infusions of Windfall Profit Tax dollars into low-income energy assistance.

The federal government's focus on direct assistance programs is a classic short-term approach to a complex problem. The money that the federal government puts into energy assistance has kept people from freezing to death—for now. It has also created a dependency and the false sense that the benefits offered through direct assistance will continue to keep pace with rising costs. LIHEAP has become an entitlement program. This has been done at the expense of a more long-term approach—conservation and alternative energy sources—that would give low-income households the ability to control their personal energy expenditures. In its attempts to balance the federal budget through budget cuts in all social programs, the Reagan administration is proposing cutbacks in *all* energy assistance programs, including the termination of weatherization assistance and the phasing out of all housing rehabilitation programs. This is concurrent with federal policies that decontrol the price of energy. In relation to weatherization, it is the U.S. Department of Energy's position that this particular program is unnecessary. "State and local governments should be responsible for decisions concerning public assistance, including weatherization assistance."[10]

This signals a significant change in the federal government's role in energy assistance. It no longer views itself as the greater equalizer, protecting the poor from rising energy prices, which are the result of its more mainstream energy and economic policies.

It signals a shift of responsibility to state and local governments and ultimately to low-income consumers, most of whom are already carrying more than their share of the responsibility for federal policy decisions. These groups are being set adrift, left to their own devices in a sea of prices, regulations, and policies over which they have little or no control but which, nonetheless, are major determinants of their daily existence.

As the federal role diminishes, many state and local units of government have sought innovative ways to respond to the plight of the low-income energy user. These are discussed in Chapter 5.

5

The Case For State Intervention

State governments responded early to the energy crisis with a variety of in-novative and experimental energy assistance programs. Like the initial federal response, many of the first state programs were crisis-oriented—designed to prevent people from freezing to death. Once states were able to assess the full impact of the energy crisis and the federal role became more defined, they began to initiate and fund programs that could better respond to specific state needs or to fill gaps in timing or service of the federal pro-grams. The movement to adopt state programs was led by those states with the coldest climates, highest energy costs, and a state government attuned to the energy-related needs of its low-income households. Oregon, Ohio, Min-nesota, and Michigan developed some of the earliest programs. Other states followed and by 1984 33 states, including the District of Columbia, were of-fering at least one type of energy assistance program—direct assistance, weatherization, or rate reduction (see Table 5.1).

Federal policies and programs have greatly shaped the state response. The Public Utility Regulatory Policy Act led many states to adopt rate-relief pro-grams, just as the RCS program led to the adoption of state conservation programs. The federal government remains the largest source of funding for energy assistance, yet state and local governments are the innovators in pro-gram design and implementation.

The recent shift to block grants and the decline in federal funding for social/domestic programs have far-reaching implications for state energy assistance programs. States have more discretion and responsibility in the allocation of diminishing federal energy assistance dollars. Moreover, federal budget cuts increase the pressure on state governments to provide their own funding for energy assistance.

Yet state resources are also shrinking. Many state programs are threatened by state fiscal constraints brought about by a shrinking tax base, increased unemployment, and pressure to cut taxes. These factors not only threaten

Table 5.1

State Energy Assistance Programs by Type and Year, 1979, 1981, 1984

State	1979 DA	WN	RT*	1981 DA	WN	RT*	1984 DA	WN	RT*
Alabama									1
Alaska				1	2			3	1
Arizona		1							1
Arkansas									1
California			1		2	1		1	1
Colorado			1	1	1		2	2	
Connecticut	2			2	1		2	4	
Dist. of Columbia			1				1		
Delaware					1				
Georgia			1						
Hawaii					1			1	
Illinois						1			1
Indiana	2						1		
Iowa			1			1		1	1
Kansas							1		
Kentucky	1	1							
Maine			2		1			1	
Maryland					1			1	
Massachusetts			2	1		2	2	2	8
Michigan	1	1	1	1	1	1	3	3	
Minnesota			3		4	1		3	1
Missouri			2	1					
Montana									2
New Hampshire						1			3
New Jersey				1			2	1	
New Mexico				1	1		1		
New York			2	2				1	
North Carolina		1	3			2			2
North Dakota					1				
Ohio	1		1	1	1		1	1	
Oklahoma								1	1
Oregon	1	3			2			1	
Pennsylvania	1								
Rhode Island			2	1		1			1
South Carolina						1			1
Utah			1			1			1
Vermont									1
Washington									1
West Virginia						1			2
Wisconsin	1		1			1		1	1
Wyoming	1							1	
No. of states with programs	9	4	17	11	14	13	9	19	20
States with any type of program		23			27			33	

*Many of these rate programs are counted by the number of utility companies participating which inflates the number of programs.

Note: DA = Direct Assistance; WN = Weatherization; RT = Rate.

Source: Derived from Jean H. Standish, Vonna M. McDonald, Robert R. Myers and David C. Sweet, *Trends Report of Energy Assistance Programs in the Fifty States, 1979–1984,* Occasional Paper No. 11, The National Regulatory Research Institute, Columbus, Ohio, December 1985, pp. 51–56, 61–67, 71–72. Reprinted with permission.

the continuation of existing energy assistance programs but also make it more difficult for states to continue their active role in developing new programs to fill the ever-widening gap in federal energy assistance.

As the federal government retreats from the funding of energy assistance programs, the task of defining the appropriate state role in energy assistance takes on increased importance and urgency. This chapter examines how states have responded to the energy crisis and offers insights into the appropriate state role.

THE EMERGENCE OF STATE PROGRAMS

As part of on-going research into the problem of energy and the poor, the College of Urban Affairs at Cleveland State University conducted a two-year research effort to study exemplary state–initiated and state–funded energy assistance programs. (For detailed information on these programs, see CSU, College of Urban Affairs, "Energy and the Poor: Alternative Non-Rate Structure Programs," May 1981.) The purpose of this study was to provide information about the effective use of scarce state resources to meet the energy assistance needs of low-income households.

Cleveland State University also conducted three surveys—in 1979, 1981, and 1984—to determine the level of state involvement in energy assistance. The findings of these studies offer insights into the development of state initiated energy assistance programs.

As were their federal counterparts, successful state energy assistance programs were initiated largely through the efforts of either a strong interest group, the commitment of a strong individual, or supportive state legislators. A prerequisite for passage of state energy programs was a constituency supportive of energy assistance or a general consensus that an energy problem existed.

The conditions for the growth of an energy assistance constituency at the state level were more practical than political in nature. Rising energy costs and their impact on the poor, a cold climate, the cost of importing large amounts of energy, and, in the case of weatherization programs, an older, uninsulated housing stock were the major impetuses behind state energy programs. Consequently, those states with the coldest climates and highest energy costs were the leaders in energy assistance. More recently, energy-producing states have begun to invest some of their energy profits in conservation activities for low-income households.

State programs have been initiated in a variety of ways, many from the bottom up. Successful programs run by neighborhood organizations, agency staff, or utility companies were adopted as statewide models. Others came from the top down through either the state legislatures or the state Public Utility Commissions (PUCs) often in response to lobbying from various stakeholders. Yet all depended for their success on a supportive executive branch.

Regulators tend to view the problem of energy and the poor as an economic/energy problem, while legislators tend to view it as a social problem. Programs developed by the public utility commission are administered in most cases by utility companies and involve some form of rate relief, shut-off moratorium, or utility–funded weatherization programs. Legislative solutions tend to be linked with other state programs and are administered through such state agencies as housing authorities, welfare departments, development departments, and in some cases tax departments. Rarely are energy assistance programs run through state energy offices.

In some states the question of providing energy assistance to the poor became a political football. All three branches of state government acknowledged the severity of the problem but none wanted to deal with it. One regulator described it as a badminton game "where the legislature passes it back to us and we pass it back to the legislature and nobody deals with the problem."[1]

This batting back and forth of the problem is a direct result of its underlying complexity. Those with a legitimate stake in energy policy decisions were often unable to reach consensus among themselves, much less communicate clear signals to state decision makers about appropriate solutions to the problem.

Regulators sometimes took a lead role through default—legislators were reluctant to act on energy assistance issues, yet people were freezing. Regulators responded by imposing moratoria on utility disconnections in the winter months or by requiring the companies to implement lifeline rates.

Gormley found that

given legislative inertia, public utility regulators must either ignore social equity considerations altogether (a callous choice) or incorporate such considerations into pricing decisions (which might be deemed discriminatory pricing by the courts) . . . there is no excuse for legislative failure to address questions of social justice.[2]

States with high utility rates and appointed, highly professional commissions were most likely also to have a high level of public intervention in PUC proceedings. In these states, there was a greater level of innovation in dealing with energy assistance. In three such states—Massachusetts, Michigan, and New York—the state public utility commissioners adopted time-of-day rates and interruptible service rates and Massachusetts and Michigan adopted lifeline rates.

The Michigan Public Service Commission went much further. It took the lead in comprehensively redesigning the state energy assistance programs to ensure that all customers would have basic energy service at an affordable price. This involved gaining the support of the governor and passage of a complex bill by the legislature. The resulting Energy Assurance Program is multifaceted and includes both direct assistance and weatherization. It involves the utility companies, the state social service agency, the state community service agency, the state housing authority, and the treasury department in administering programs. It is supported by both state and federal funds and its passage required a major legislative effort, spearheaded by the commission and the utilities. This is the most comprehensive energy assistance effort found at the state level.[3]

More typically, the legislature and PUC shared responsibility for addressing the problem, not through any coordinated or planned effort but more as a result of who picked up the ball on what issues. For example, in Ohio a program for the elderly and disabled, the Ohio Energy Credits Program, was passed in 1977 through the initiative and hard work of one state legislator. The program offers discounts on utility bills and is administered by the state Department of Taxation. At about the same time, the PUC imposed a moratorium on utility shut-offs during the winter months. Later, in 1984, the Commission adopted a special payment program for low-income households, the Percentage-of-Income Payment Plan (see Chapter 7) and is considering a utility-financed weatherization program as part of an ambitious effort to develop "long-term solutions" to the low-income energy assistance problem. As a result of an initiative taken in the executive branch, the state also has several weatherization programs. While Ohio's programs have some of the same components as Michigan's the important distinction in terms of policy development is that Ohio has no overall strategy, nor does it have one actor who has taken a lead role.

The type of program that states chose to implement—weatherization, direct assistance, rate reduction, or a combination of the three—depended upon the circumstances of the particular state. In general, direct assistance programs originated to deal with the emergency situation of people freezing to death. These state programs were designed to fill a gap in federal programs, to serve an underserved group such as the elderly, or in response to uncertainties in federal funding.

The rationale behind weatherization programs differed depending on the type of program considered. As opposed to direct assistance programs, weatherization programs, in general, were the result of a more studied and rational effort and were less crisis-oriented. In several cases they were tied into statewide housing programs.

Rate programs, for the most part, were initiated in response to PURPA (see Chapter 4). However, some states with progressive, socially oriented public utility commissions adopted rate programs prior to the federal mandate.

A few energy-rich states—New Mexico, Alaska, and North Dakota—used their "windfall" oil profits to assist those in need. However, these states were more likely to develop conservation-oriented programs than direct assistance programs.

Direct Assistance

Many state direct assistance programs were initiated in response to funding delays in the federal programs, to serve an underserved group such as the elderly, or in response to uncertainties in federal funding. In the years of CIP, EEAP, and SCIP, when federal funds were not available until after or late in the heating season, states often implemented their own one-time emergency assistance programs to help their residents in the interim, until federal funds were available. In an attempt to retain state funding for direct assistance, the federal government prohibited states from substituting federal LIHEAP funds for state funds in state–run programs. Yet many states began to phase out their early direct assistance programs and to develop new supplementary programs—designed to serve persons just above the federal cutoff or to provide additional funds—as the federal program grew more reliable. The CSU surveys support this finding. In 1979 fourteen programs in ten states offered direct assistance to low-income, elderly, and disabled households. These programs are summarized in Table 5.2.

An update of the 1979 survey conducted in 1981 indicated that of the ten states that had programs in 1979 only three—Connecticut, Michigan, and Ohio—still had programs in 1981. But, by then, an additional eight states had implemented ten new programs for a total of fourteen programs (see Table 5.3).

Between 1981 and 1984, only two states entered the direct assistance arena and four states terminated their 1981 programs (see Table 5.4). Pressure on states to fund new direct assistance programs fell off as a result of the less-crisis-oriented atmosphere, the introduction of a new federal source of funds (oil overcharge funds), and the continuation of existing state–funded programs.

Table 5.5 compares the state programs over the three survey years. Only Connecticut, Michigan, and Ohio demonstrated a continuous commitment to state-funded direct assistance programs since 1979. It is significant, however, that total funding levels for these programs have increased in almost every state (see Table 5.5).

No states supplemented the federal program in 1979, but by 1984 four states were adding their own money to expand the assistance that could be provided. This is the result of two changes in the LIHEAP program: the continuity of funding and the flexibility awarded to the states in designing their own programs.

The 1981 update also noted an increase in the number of programs providing direct aid to recipients of Aid to Families with Dependent Children, General Assistance (GA), or other public assistance. Michigan was the first state to set aside a portion of an AFDC or GA recipient's monthly payment and pay this directly to the recipient's utility company. This program, the Voluntary Heating Fuel Program was a pilot program and required special

Table 5.2
1979 Direct Aid Program Components

State	Type	Eligibility	Benefit
Connecticut	Cash payment	Low income	$250
	Federal program supplement	Low income	NA
Indiana	Vendor tax reduction	Low-income elderly & other low income	Heating bill reduction
	Vendor payment	Low income	$250
Kentucky	Two-party check	Low-income elderly & disabled	Varies
Michigan	Vendor payment	Low-income elderly & other low income	$200
	Tax credit	Income & size of household	$370
Ohio	Vendor or cash payment	Low-income elderly & disabled	$125 or 25-30% heating bill reduction
Oregon	Elderly rate relief	Low-income elderly	$50
Pennsylvania	Vendor tax reduction	Low-income elderly	15-35% utility bill reduction
Wisconsin	Loans	Low income	$200
Wyoming	Cash payment	Low-income elderly	$500

Note: NA = Not Available

Source: Derived from Jean H. Standish, Vonna M. McDonald, Robert R. Myers and David C. Sweet, *Trends Report of Energy Assistance Programs in the Fifty States, 1979–1984,* Occasional Paper No. 11, The National Regulatory Research Institute, Columbus, Ohio, December 1985, p. 51. Reprinted with permission.

permission from the U.S. Department of Health and Human Services (HHA). The program proved to be successful and was studied in depth by CSU's Energy Program. New York enacted a similar program in September 1981.

These direct-aid programs, in effect, make the state welfare office the guarantor of welfare recipients' utility bills. New York also adopted a program to increase monthly welfare benefits by 15 percent as a home energy grant, to cover increased utility bills. (While these states have recognized the need to *increase* welfare payments to cover increasing utility bills, the federal government has proposed a way to *decrease* welfare and food stamp payments by counting energy assistance as income in determining eligibility and benefit levels. For food stamp recipients, $3.00 to $5.25 worth of food stamps would be lost for every $10.00 of energy assistance received. For welfare recipients it would mean a dollar-for-dollar trade-off.)

Despite the increase in state funding for direct assistance programs since 1979, the federal government overwhelmingly remains the major provider of funds. As the following table of federal and state direct assistance funding

Table 5.3
1981 Direct Aid Program Components

State	Type	Eligibility	Benefit
Alaska	Utility co. subsidy	Rural electric companies	Lower residential rates
Colorado	Tax credit	Low-income elderly	$160
Connecticut	Vendor payment	Low income	$150
	Vendor payment	Low income crisis situation	$150
Massachusetts	Federal program supplement	Low income	$325
Michigan	Vendor payment	GA & ADC recipients	Heating bill payment
Missouri	Vendor payment	Low-income elderly & disabled	$150
New Jersey	Vendor payment	Low-income elderly	$125
New Mexico	Vendor or cash payment	Low income	$400
New York	Cash payment	Public assistance recipients	15% benefit
	Vendor payment	Public assistance recipients	Utility bill payment
Ohio	Vendor or cash payment	Low-income elderly or disabled	$125 or 25-30% heating bill reduction
Rhode Island	Vendor payment	Elderly & crisis	$100

Source: Derived from Jean H. Standish, Vonna M. McDonald, Robert R. Myers and David C. Sweet, *Trends Report of Energy Assistance Programs in the Fifty States, 1979-1984,* Occasional Paper No. 11, The National Regulatory Research Institute, Columbus, Ohio, December 1985, p. 53. Reprinted with permission.

levels (excluding energy tax credits) indicates, of the nearly $2.3 billion spent on direct assistance programs in 1984, just less than 8 percent came from the states:

Source	*Funding (billions)*
HHS-LIHEAP	2.075
DOE-oil overcharge funds	.018
State funds	.191
	2.284

State governments simply do not have the financial resources to take on a much larger role in energy assistance. Their strength lies in their ability to use the federal dollars innovatively and creatively to best serve the needs of the low- and moderate-income households in their states. Most states have responded to the challenge of the LIHEAP block grant by taking more re-

Table 5.4
1984 Direct Aid Program Components

State	Type	Eligibility	Benefit
Colorado	Tax credit	Low-income elderly	$160
	Utility allowance	Low-income elderly	$120
Connecticut	Vendor payment	Moderate-income elderly & disabled	$400
	Emergency program	Low-income emergency	$200
District of Columbia	Supplemental payment*	AFDC recipient	$1,200
Indiana	Supplemental vendor credit	Low income & elderly	$263
Massachusetts	Supplemental payment	Low income	Percentage of bill
	Heating aid	One or two person, low-income elderly, disabled	$325
Michigan	Income-tax credit	Low income	$502
	Supplemental vendor payment & cash payment	ADC recipients	$900
	Additional ADC check	ADC recipients	$172
New Jersey	Emergency vendor payment	Low income & low-income elderly & disabled	Clothing, blankets $200
New Mexico	Supplemental	Low income	Based on matrix
Ohio	Vendor or cash payment	Low-income elderly & disabled	25-30% heating bill reduction

*Supplemental payment indicates that state funds are used to supplement the LIHEAP funds.

Source: Derived from Jean H. Standish, Vonna M. McDonald, Robert R. Myers and David C. Sweet, *Trends Report of Energy Assistance Programs in the Fifty States, 1979-1984,* Occasional Paper No. 11, The National Regulatory Research Institute, Columbus, Ohio, December 1985, p. 55. Reprinted with permission.

sponsibility in designing their programs. As the states gain more experience, some have begun to leverage scarce state and federal dollars with private and utility company dollars to expand the scope of their programs.

Weatherization

Perhaps because of the federal government's reluctance to provide low-income weatherization and conservation programs, states have taken a stronger role in this area and are involved in a variety of weatherization programs: grants and loans, tax credits, information, utility–sponsored loans, supplements to the federal program, and rebates.

Table 5.5
Direct Aid Programs—
Total State Funding Levels, 1979, 1981, 1984

State	1979	1981	1984
Alaska		NA	
Colorado		$ 3,400,000	$ 7,923,516
Connecticut	$ 2,355,000	1,100,000	1,500,000
District of Columbia			2,662,000
Indiana	32,000,000		6,741,100
Kentucky	5,000,000		
Massachusetts		20,500,000	17,000,000
Michigan	38,000,000	28,500,000	57,700,000
Missouri		1,400,000	
New Jersey		21,900,000	55,234,000
New Mexico		1,000,000	1,088,000
New York		NA	
Ohio	46,000,000	37,300,000	42,000,000
Oregon	7,000,000		
Pennsylvania	NA		
Rhode Island		40,000	
Wisconsin	NA		
Wyoming	2,500,000		
Total	$132,855,000	$115,140,000	$191,848,616

Note: NA = Not Available

Source: Derived from Jean H. Standish, Vonna M. McDonald, Robert R. Myers and David C. Sweet, *Trends Report of Energy Assistance Programs in the Fifty States, 1979–1984,* Occasional Paper No. 11, The National Regulatory Research Institute, Columbus, Ohio, December 1985, pp. 51–56. Reprinted with permission.

Not counting utility–sponsored programs that are discussed in Chapter 7, four states offered six weatherization/conservation programs to their low-income households in 1979. By 1981, the number of programs more than tripled to 20 programs offered by 14 states. By 1984, 19 states had 31 programs that provided weatherization and conservation assistance. Table 5.6 illustrates this steady increase in state involvement in weatherization/ conservation.

As opposed to direct assistance programs, the development of state weatherization programs, in general, was less crisis–oriented. For example, in a well-studied approach, Minnesota and Michigan included weatherization as an integral part of their home improvement programs in light of evidence that energy–related expenditures were taking an increasingly larger portion of the low- and moderate–income family's housing budget and were having a major adverse impact on the family's ability to meet monthly expenses and maintain property.

Minnesota enacted energy conservation standards to encourage residential energy savings and to limit the state's vulnerability to fossil fuel short-

Table 5.6
State Weatherization/Conservation Programs by Type and Year, 1979, 1981, 1984

State	Grants			Low/No Interest Loans			Tax Credits			Cash Rebate		
	79	81	84	79	81	84	79	81	84	79	81	84
Alaska		1	1			2						
California							1	1		1		
Colorado			1				1	1				
Connecticut			1		1	3						
Delaware											1	
Hawaii							1	1				
Iowa			1									
Kansas								1				
Kentucky	1											
Maine			1	1								
Maryland					1	1						
Massachusetts			1			1						
Michigan	1		2	1		1						
Minnesota		1	2	3		1						
New Jersey						1						
New Mexico		1										
New York			1									
North Carolina							1					
North Dakota			1									
Ohio			1						1			
Oklahoma			1									
Oregon				1	1	1	1	1		1		1
Wisconsin						1						
Wyoming			1									
Total	2	5	13	1	8	12	2	4	5	1	2	1

Summary: 1979 - 6 programs, 4 states
1981 - 19 programs, 14 states
1984 - 31 programs, 19 states

Source: Derived from Jean H. Standish, Vonna M. McDonald, Robert R. Myers, and David C. Sweet, *Trends Report of Energy Assistance Programs in the Fifty States, 1979–1984,* Occasional Paper No. 11, The National Regulatory Research Institute, Columbus, Ohio, December 1985, pp. 61, 62, 64. Reprinted with permission.

ages. The standards apply to all homes and are not specifically geared to low-income households.

A closer examination of the type of weatherization/conservation programs reveals that the majority of new programs offer grants and loans. The funds spent by states for grants, which serve the lowest income households, increased only slightly, from $26.23 million in 1981 to $31.34 million in 1984, but the number of grant programs increased dramatically from 2 in 1979 to 13 in 1984. All grant programs were funded through the states' general funds. Loan programs, on the other hand, are most often financed through the sale of bonds and require a smaller initial outlay by the states.

The 1984 survey found that more than twice as many states (19) are involved in financing weatherization/conservation programs as direct assistance programs (9 states). While pressure on states to fund direct assistance has fallen off with the relative stability of the federal program, the pressure to fund weatherization has increased for several reasons. Federal funding uncertainties are a prime force behind lobbying efforts to promote state-funded conservation. Of the 13 grant programs in 1984, 9 were supplements to federal funds. However, an equally important factor is the growing awareness among stakeholders that direct assistance needs will continue to grow and that the only way to stem this growth is through weatherization/ conservation. It represents a movement toward a more rational approach to energy assistance policy, at least on the part of state governments. A third factor behind the growing number of state programs, and this applies most directly to the loan programs, is the close linkage between weatherization and home improvements and rehabilitation. Both are often funded through the same administrative mechanism, often through the same program, and are regarded as an appropriate function for state government.

State Program Administration

Combining energy assistance programs with ongoing housing (for weatherization) and income maintenance (for direct assistance) programs at the state level yielded significant administrative benefits:

- It minimized administrative costs by eliminating the need to establish a separate administering entity.
- It ensured the continuation of the energy component of the program as long as the other component of the program was funded.
- It facilitated the development of new programs to fill gaps in the existing program. For example, the Minnesota Home Improvement Grant program was developed to serve the state's lowest income homeowners, a group that the existing loan program did not serve.
- It utilized the capacity of existing agencies. For example, the Ohio Energy Credits Program was able to utilize existing administrative and service delivery mechanisms of the Ohio Department of Taxation. Similarly, programs can be administered by utility companies without placing an administrative burden on the state. (See Chapter 7 for a discussion of utilities' role in energy assistance.)

State Program Funding

State programs are funded through a variety of sources ranging from state general funds to private contributions. Home improvement loan programs, such as those in Minnesota and Michigan, which combine home improvements with weatherization improvements, are funded by a combination of mortgage revenue bond sales and general state appropriations. This enables the state to raise relatively large sums of money with a small initial outlay of state funds and to make loans affordable to low- and moderate-income homeowners. However, the Mortgage Subsidy Bond Tax Act of 1980 placed many restrictions on the use of bond proceeds and impacted both Minnesota's and Michigan's programs. In addition, high interest rates and increased competition from savings and loans affected the states' ability to sell bonds. As a result many of the program elements in both states underwent substantial changes. The ability to serve the state's lowest income households through this type of program is deeply affected by cutbacks in state funds. Since the interest rate on home improvement loans is subsidized by state funds, cutbacks in this area are likely to lead to an increase in interest rates in the loans.

State conservation programs still rely heavily on federal discretionary funds (oil overcharge money and HUD Solar Bank money) and general funds to finance programs.

THE FUTURE OF STATE PROGRAMS

The division of responsibility between the federal and state government in the provision of all social programs, including energy assistance, is in transition as the Reagan administration strives to implement its "New Federalism." The shift in responsibility affects administration, implementation, and, to some extent, financing of these programs.

States that have a track record of commitment to low-income energy assistance have continued existing programs and, in some cases, implemented new programs. These have traditionally been the states in the industrial Northeast and Midwest regions—states with the highest energy costs, the highest unemployment rates, and therefore the least capacity to fund new programs. Yet these states have the highest stake in energy assistance.

The federal government's reliance on price to spur conservation, coupled with its continued attempts to eliminate all funding for weatherization assistance, is taking its toll. States continue to implement programs, yet they lack the financial resources of the federal government to fund them.

Those states that have demonstrated a commitment to energy assistance are likely to continue to provide assistance but fiscal constraints may force them to cut back eligibility requirements or reduce benefits. However, other states have little or no commitment to energy assistance and it is unclear how they will react to their new responsibilities. A task force of governors was appointed by the National Governor's Association on the administration's "New Federalism" proposal. As the National Consumer Law Center reports, one of the outcomes of this Task Force's discussion raised some concerns about some states' commitments to energy assistance. Many states are anxious to take over the categorical programs, however, which obviously raises questions about what services states would in reality provide, and whether the country would become even more of a checkerboard in providing widely varying services, depending simply on where one lives.[4]

If past experience is any indication, these concerns are well founded. An examination of the states' records with block grants and their longer history with the AFDC program are revealing.

The LIHEAP block grant contains a provision that up to 10 percent of funds can be transferred to another block grant. Information presented at various congressional hearings on block grants indicates that in the program's first year 18 to 20 states transferred the maximum allowable 10 percent of their energy assistance funds into other block grants and no funds were transferred into energy assistance from other block grants.[5] In 1984, $90 million were transferred to other block grants.

The AFDC record shows wide variation in average payments among the states. In general, about 55 percent of AFDC funds come from the federal government, one-third from the state, and local governments pay the rest. Eligibility standards and the level of benefits are left to the states, much as they are under the energy assistance block grant, which set maximum levels only. The states are free to set benefit levels to reflect need and can make them more (but not less) restrictive than the federal guidelines dictate. However, the wide variations raise questions as to whether some states are actually meeting existing needs. In 1984, LIHEAP payments as a percent of the average low-income household's energy expenditures ranged from a low of 6 percent in New Mexico to 58 percent in North Dakota. In 39 states, less than 30 percent of the average low-income family's home energy bill was covered by LIHEAP.[6]

THE LOCAL ROLE

The decentralization of federal energy assistance programs represents a return to the origins of these programs, many of which were initiated at the local level through Community Action Agencies. The local role in energy assistance has long been that of the broker—matching federal, state, and local financial resources with local needs (although the needs are always greater than the resources). Local government is also the service provider for many state and federal programs. Thus the quality of service in any locality is largely the responsibility of the local service provider. Within the applicable program guidelines, local agencies tailor available programs to best meet the needs of local constituents.

Consequently, the range and quality of energy assistance available in a given locality vary widely both within and across states. Most localities have had their hands full with the administration of the federal weatherization and direct assistance programs and with trying to control internal energy costs. However, other localities have encouraged innovation by community and neighborhood groups, resulting in a wealth of programs funded by sources ranging from fully public to fully private.

The local role in energy assistance is much more visible than either the state or federal role and, as a result, many people view energy assistance as a local problem. This is particularly true of weatherization/conservation and, in fact, most locally originated programs focus on conservation, leaving direct assistance to the state and federal governments. Energy conservation fits in well with other local responsibilities for housing, transportation, and economic development. Consequently, energy conservation can be successfully integrated into home improvement and rehabilitation programs, new construction codes, zoning ordinances, land-use plans, and other community and economic development activities. Most cities have energy offices that coordinate these activities.

Local governments have been active in no-cost/low-cost programs that can result in large savings for a relatively small cost. These programs involve energy audits, caulking and weather stripping, and minor home repairs. For example, the City of Cleveland Department of Community Development offers several workshops that provide do-it-yourself weatherization kits and hands-on installation demonstrations. This program is supported by the City's Community Development Block Grant.

Other local efforts include low-interest conservation loans and grants, fuel cooperatives, educational programs, and energy conservation standards. Local governments are also involved in the production of alternative energy sources. This reduces the overall cost of energy to all local residents, which indirectly and permanently assists low-income households. Making a locality more self-sufficient and reducing the outflow of energy dollars also contributes to economic development. District heating systems and solar and wind power are the most common.

Local government cannot act alone in this area. A variety of groups can provide technical assistance and research and development activities. For example, various local neighborhood development organizations, including the Center for Neighborhood Development at Cleveland State University, work with neighborhood organizations and city governments to promote renewable energy sources and conservation.

Local governments draw upon resources available from private corporations, charitable foundations, and utility companies to finance local efforts. The Ford Foundation took a leading role in fostering neighborhood energy conservation programs nationwide as did the Standard Oil Company's Office of Corporate Contributions. The most successful local efforts are spearheaded by individuals or groups committed to energy conservation and able to attract these resources.

State programs have served a very important role in the provision of energy assistance. While the federal government has provided the bulk of funds for energy assistance, the states have been in the forefront in developing creative programs. State programs are characterized by a great deal of experimentation. Programs are constantly evolving. As a result, there is no definite formula to ensure a successful energy assistance program. What works well in one state may not work in another.

The shift at the federal funding level to block grants has increased the pressure on states to develop and finance their own programs. More important, as states are left with much of the policy-making and evaluation responsibilities previously assumed by the federal government, they become the pivotal level of government with regard to energy assistance.

Increasing competition for limited state and federal funds will necessitate careful planning and analysis by state officials to document the need for and the effectiveness of energy assistance. The block grants allow the states the discretion to tailor programs (within certain constraints) to their specific needs.

Although the crisis mentality surrounding energy seems to be decreasing, the price of energy is not and the need for assistance is increasing. High unemployment rates and the continued high gas prices will make it more difficult for low- and moderate-income households to keep up with their heating bills.

The impact of overall federal energy policy has been uneven in terms of energy prices in different regions of the country. However, in a statement to reporters on November 19, 1981, President Reagan "disclaimed any federal role in equalizing resources between rich and poor states (in general) and said that citizens of distressed places could 'vote with their feet' by leaving."[7]

The need for federal intervention in resolving the problem of energy and the poor is clear. Very simply, if it is federal government policy to intervene in the production, distribution, and pricing of energy, then it is the federal government's responsibility to equalize the impacts and to protect those who are penalized as a result of that policy—that is, the low- and fixed-income—regardless of President Reagan's insistence that low-income people can "vote with their feet." The big question then is not *whether* government should intervene but rather *how*. The "how" question can best be answered at the state level. However, none of the actors—federal, state, and local government; energy producers and distributors; consumers; advocates—have been able to agree on whether this policy should be designed to conserve energy, help the poor deal with the crisis brought about by rapidly rising fuel costs, supplement inadequate welfare benefits, ensure a minimum or life-sustaining supply of energy, or promote jobs. Because of the lack of focus or priorities, programs have been developed to do a little bit of each. While they may have started out with good intentions, none has succeeded in accomplishing its objective. The programs are underfunded, uncoordinated, and unable to meet even the most basic needs.

The result is a quagmire of programs that are difficult to administer on the one hand and equally difficult to access on the other. There is no clear delineation between federal, state, and local responsibilities. By default the federal government provides the bulk of the funding, with state and localities augmenting this as their needs dictate and their resources allow. While there are national guidelines covering eligibility requirements and benefit levels, actual benefits vary from one state to another depending upon need, climate, type of fuel used, and income. There is currently no federally mandated standard of service even though one was recommended by the Fuel Oil Marketing Advisory Committee of the DOE as early as 1980. (FOMAC recommended that low-income households pay no more than 10 percent of their income on energy. Government would pick up the rest. However, if this 10 percent standard were adopted, the cost for LIHEAP would have been a little more than double what it was in 1980–81: $3.5 to $4.6 billion instead of $1.6 billion.)

Direct assistance emerged as a crisis assistance program, to fill the gap when welfare payments did not keep pace with rapidly rising energy costs. These policies have now come full circle. Proposals to count energy assistance payments as income in determining eligibility and benefit levels for AFDC and Food Stamps have the effect of substituting energy assistance for other welfare payments, thus reducing overall payments to eligible households.

Energy assistance has become a politically acceptable method of achieving income maintenance and is being funded at the expense of other welfare programs. Therefore, the value of energy assistance programs must be examined at the federal and state levels as part of the larger question of welfare and housing programs.

Without a focus, or at least a set of priorities for energy assistance, the signals that are sent to recipients often conflict. Households are told that a portion of their utility bills will be paid during the winter heating or summer cooling months. They are guaranteed a minimum level of heat whether they conserve or not. Any incentives or requirements for them to apply for weatherization programs are meaningless given the scarce dollars available and the backlogs in most states. The bulk of weatherization funds now comes from the 15 percent set-aside from the Low-Income Home Energy Assistance Program, which underlines the need for a coordinated strategy at both the policy and program level. (For 1985, the DOE Weatherization Assistance Program was funded at $191 million and the LIHEAP 15 percent set-aside amounted to $230 million.) Yet one of the greatest barriers to coordination is the dichotomy that exists in most state and federal program administrators' thinking about weatherization and direct assistance. State administrators are just beginning to regard these two separate programs as parts of an overall effort to assist low-income households in dealing with rising energy costs. As a result very little coordination exists between the two types of programs, even when they are administered by the same state agencies.

If the objective of energy assistance programs is to assist low-income households in dealing with rising energy costs, then a multifaceted approach makes more sense than paying money to households to pay bills on the one hand and to pay for weatherizing the housing of another group of households on the other hand. If no effort is made to conserve energy in the homes of those receiving direct assistance, then the federal (and in some cases state) dollars are literally going out the window and up the chimney.

Many states have advisory committees or task forces made up of representatives from utilities, consumer groups, the governor's office, and such other state agencies as housing, aging, and development that have an interest in energy. These groups have been used in planning, oversight, evaluation, outreach, and, in some cases, coordination.

As states begin to make long-term decisions about their energy assistance programs, these or similar bodies can be used as working groups to develop an overall state energy assistance strategy. By reducing duplication, setting long-term priorities, and increasing administrative efficiency, such a coordinated strategy would allow more households to be served at a higher level of benefits using fewer resources.

PART III

THE PRIVATE AND INDEPENDENT SECTOR RESPONSE

6

The Independent Sector Response

The role of the independent sector in energy assistance is smaller in scale but broader in scope than the role of the public sector. Privately financed programs are usually innovative, pilot efforts that test new approaches to the problem or address unmet needs. Most are locally oriented, designed to serve the needs of a specific group or locality. In essence, the independent sector adds the highlights to the energy assistance picture.

For the purposes of this discussion, the independent sector includes private, community, and corporate foundations and nonprofit organizations. Public utilities are considered in a separate chapter. The independent sector is involved in all types of energy assistance—direct assistance, emergency assistance, weatherization, conservation, renewable resources, technical assistance, information, and education. Because of the diversity and the local nature of many private efforts, there is little comprehensive documentation of the contribution of this important sector. Yet it is very often the trend setter in energy assistance policy.

This chapter will present an overview of private–sector intervention in energy assistance, the different vehicles for this intervention, and their relationship to larger public efforts.

Corporate and community foundations and nonprofits are involved in energy assistance at different levels. Foundations play a "behind-the-scenes" but very influential role in developing and funding special projects to meet local needs. Beyond a minimum level of oversight and evaluation by these funders, projects are administered largely by nonprofits. Nonprofits play a very visible role. Their involvement in energy is seen as an extension of their broader social and community development efforts.

CORPORATE FOUNDATIONS

Just as government must balance the interest of various constituencies in developing public programs and policies, a corporation also has constituents whose needs must be met. These constituents include stockholders, customers, employees, and the community.

Those corporations that are involved in energy assistance regard it as one part of their responsibility to the community(ies) they serve. Corporate foundations and, on a smaller scale, corporate donations programs are the vehicles used by corporations to fulfill these social responsibilities. In most cases, energy-related companies have taken the lead in energy program funding.

One reason for the predominance of energy company involvement is that corporations usually set certain priorities to guide them in funding. Programs that meet both a pressing community need and an area of interest for the company are often high priorities. Corporations are most comfortable funding programs that are highly visible, create little controversy, and have the potential to leverage other dollars—either public or private.

Because energy assistance is a relatively new, untested, and therefore potentially risky area of giving for corporations, few companies other than energy concerns have become involved. To put the corporate role in energy assistance in perspective, all corporate giving in the United States approximated $3 billion in 1983, a decade after the beginning of the "energy crisis," and only a small portion of this went for energy-related programs. While corporate involvement is on a small scale relative to government funding levels, programs funded by corporations often have far-reaching impact.

As we have said, energy corporations are the frontrunners in funding energy assistance. (This does not include utility companies, which are treated separately in Chapter 7. The term "oil companies" does not adequately describe these corporations, which now control a variety of our energy resources including coal and natural gas.) The sudden increase in energy prices, while creating a tremendous burden for many Americans, also created tremendous profits for others, particularly the owners of large energy corporations. Even though the Crude Oil Windfall Profits Tax Act of 1980 proposed to equalize some of this disparity by taxing the windfall profits and using the money raised through these taxes for energy assistance, the energy corporations were still left with record-breaking profits. A few responded by increasing their corporate contributions, primarily to improve their public relations and offset the negative image created by their sudden rise in profits at the expense of consumers.

For example, the Standard Oil Company is an energy company headquartered in Cleveland and is the largest holder of domestic proved crude oil reserves, through its ownership of leases on the North Slope of Alaska. In 1984, the Standard Oil Company donated almost $17 million to support programs in localities where it has employees and facilities. As early as 1981, it took the initiative to respond to critical community problems, one of which was defined as the vulnerability of low-income people to rising home heating costs, in keeping with the company's energy orientation. In 1982 the company's "Urban Energy Program" was launched. By March 1984 it had contributed over $1 million to nonprofits to promote energy conservation and help people trim energy bills. Much of this money went directly to the Cleveland area and contributed to making the city's nonprofits some of the most sophisticated in the country in terms of energy assistance. It also encouraged other local givers to fund energy-related projects.

The Standard Oil Company views its program as a demonstration of cost-effective measures for retrofitting low-income housing. According to Dr. Lance C. Buhl, manager of corporate contributions for Standard Oil, "Controlling energy costs is seen as an effective tool in the broader self help movement taking place in neighborhoods across the country."[1] Standard Oil's experience is representative of the way most large corporations view their corporate giving programs. Funding is seen as an important part in a public/private venture to assist low-income people in finding new, effective approaches to local problems.

Other examples of corporate involvement in energy include the Ford Motor Company and GM Foundations, which provided operating support to the Alliance to Save Energy, a group based in Washington, D.C., committed to exploring the costs and benefits of various conservation measures for low-income housing. The "Blue-Chip In" project in Baltimore mobilized more than two dozen corporations to provide funds for a number of projects to help the poor, including the weatherization of houses.

PRIVATE AND COMMUNITY FOUNDATIONS

Private and community foundations are often partners with corporations in funding energy assistance efforts. As is characteristic of their involvement in other social programs, these foundations prefer to fund innovative solutions to highly visible problems. Projects that build up the capacity of community organizations and have the potential to spin-off and become free-standing, self-reliant programs are good prospects for foundation support.

However, at the same time that energy assistance providers are looking more and more to the independent sector for support, foundations are facing cuts in the level of contributions (or new endowments) that help keep them going. The Economic Recovery Act of 1981 cut the maximum individual income tax level from 70 to 50 percent. More recent tax reform proposals would cut this even further. Foundations fear that this will reduce the level of giving, particularly the large endowments, as people seek other tax shelters for their money.[2] Further, a study conducted by Yale University's Program on Non-Profit Organizations and the Council on Foundations found a significant decrease in the creation of large foundations (with assets of $1 million or more) since 1969 as a result of changes in tax laws.[3]

The decline in support for foundations, both existing and new, may prevent them from becoming more involved in energy assistance, which represents an entry into new, untested ground. In general, foundations are also hesitant to fund capital projects or operating expenses of nonprofits, which precludes many areas of energy conservation assistance.

The Ford and the John A. Hartford Foundations have been very active in the area of energy assistance. In early 1982 the Hartford Foundation expanded its activities and made grants to five communities in New England and Colorado to promote energy efficiency with voluntary citizen participation. The Ford Foundation's interest in the problems of energy and the poor grew out of its broader interest in the economic future of energy. After sponsoring a large project to examine America's energy future, Ford realized it had virtually ignored the problems the study's recommendations would cause for the poor. As a result, it funded a subsequent study of state-funded alternative, nonrate energy assistance programs, undertaken by the Energy Program at Cleveland State University, College of Urban Affairs, and a study of neighborhood initiatives, undertaken by the Civic Action Institute. In addition to research, Ford has become involved on a project level. For example, it funded a program in Hartford, Connecticut, to train community leaders and plan programs to prevent housing abandonment because of rising energy costs. It also established a demonstration program that awarded grants to five cities for neighborhood energy conservation projects. The demonstration program had three objectives: (1) weatherizing low-income owner-occupied housing, (2) preserving residential neighborhoods, and (3) building nonprofit organizational capacity.

One of these was awarded to the Cleveland Center for Neighborhood Development (CCND) at CSU's College of Urban Affairs. CCND is using the grant for a comprehensive energy conservation effort to

train neighborhood coordinators and existing support programs, to stimulate the efforts of the local utility companies in their energy conservation efforts, to provide energy audits for low-income residents, and to make possible low-interest loans and grants to homeowners for energy improvements.[4]

Examples of efforts by other foundations include:

- Grants from the George Gund Foundation in Cleveland to neighborhood groups to develop self-help projects in the fields of housing, food and energy.
- A grant from the Indianapolis Foundation to Indianapolis Settlements to convert two neighborhood settlement houses from oil to gas heat.
- A grant from the McKnight Foundation in Minnesota to a local community council for start-up funds for a neighborhood energy conservation program.

• A grant from the Rockefeller Brothers Fund in New York for an energy conservation manual for old law tenements in New York City.

One area of energy assistance in which both corporations and foundations are heavily involved is the weatherization of buildings of nonprofit organizations (NPOs). These include religious, health, housing, educational, arts and cultural, and social welfare agencies. Most of these agencies serve large low-income populations.

These programs are designed to cut energy costs for NPOs at a time when increasingly large portions of their operating budgets are going for utilities and government spending for social programs, while the arts and education are being cut. The objective of the programs is to free up money that would be spent on energy for use in social service delivery. Many NPOs' buildings are energy inefficient and administrators have little incentive to conserve, even if it does mean saving scarce dollars.

This lack of incentives is the result of a combination of limited technical, financial, and organizational skills, limited access to capital, ignorance about conservation efficiency, and fear of risk. Several foundations, including both the New York and the Chicago Community Trusts, have set up Energy Conservation Funds (ECFs) designed to assist agencies to identify, finance, and implement energy conservation measures, overcome the barriers to conservation, and to secure relief from the "energy cost-squeeze."

Private energy corporations have taken the lead in several cities in initiating these programs. The Amoco Foundation, the giving arm of the Amoco Corporation, set up a program in Chicago that is targeted to neighborhood-based nonprofit organizations. The Standard Oil Company has also funded an ECF, together with other local utilities and corporations in Cleveland.

These programs benefit low-income households only indirectly, at best. By enabling NPOs to reduce energy consumption, they save on operating expenses, thus reducing the burden on their funding sources. Presumably this money can then be spent on service provision. However, it is not clear that the benefits ever reach the clients in the form of improved services. As an incentive for NPOs to carry out the conservation measures prescribed by the audits, these programs often enable the agencies to retain a portion of the savings (or costs avoided), which they can then spend according to their needs. However, participation rates have not been as high as had been expected, even with the shared savings plan.

Private, community, and corporate foundations have contributed to the nation's overall energy assistance policy by funding innovative, small-scale projects that can leverage other sources of funding and build the capacity of community-based organizations to respond to the energy-related needs of their neighborhoods. Some of these programs, like that of the Standard Oil Company and the Ford Foundation's demonstration program, were designed to test new ideas that could then be replicated on a larger scale through the use of public funds.

NONPROFITS

Nonprofits are the primary service delivery mechanism for programs funded by foundations and corporations. Because of their small scale and local nature, these programs are generally the most innovative and responsive to local needs. However, these characteristics that make the nonprofits responsive to local needs also make them inappropriate for dealing with the broader areas of energy assistance policy such as direct assistance and large-scale weatherization. These latter programs are too costly and too broad to be handled by nonprofits.

Nonprofits act as a link between the public and private sectors. Their strengths lie in their ability to draw on diverse sources of funds, both government and private, and their access to committed volunteers and in-kind contributions, both of which reduce administrative costs. Further, they are not subject to the constraints of government agencies. Their grass-roots base gives them credibility in the neighborhoods they serve, which government agencies often lack. However, they are limited by their lack of access to capital.

Nonprofits are involved in a wide variety of energy assistance activities, including energy conservation, experimenting with alternative energy sources, protesting rate increases, outreach, education, technical assistance, and audits. Cooperatives are one form of NPO involvement in the purchase of bulk fuel, weatherization materials, and solar equipment.

The Portland (Maine) Wood Fuel Co-op offers an example of how a neighborhood organization drew together public and private resources in response to local needs. The fuel co-op, which began in 1979, is funded by a combination of grants from the U.S. ACTION program, which cover administrative costs, and bank financing, which covers the purchase of wood. The co-op was implemented in an effort to hold down utility prices by reducing demand through the use of alternative sources, that is, wood. It was able to take advantage of Portland's abundant wood supply. Members were entitled to price discounts in exchange for processing the wood. Special provisions accommodated the elderly and handicapped who could not work in the co-op.[5]

In Cleveland, neighborhood-based nonprofit organizations are assisted by grants from the George Gund Foundation, the Cleveland Foundation, the Standard Oil Company's Office of Corporate Contributions, the Ford Foundation, and technical assistance from CSU's Center for Neighborhood Development to weatherize homes and retrofit heating systems in their neighborhoods. Examples of programs include a home weatherization program, a program to test alternative approaches to energy conservation, a furnace retrofit program, a neighborhood energy audit program, and a business that manufactures energy-efficient windows using neighborhood-based labor. Using foundation grants, neighborhood organizations are able to leverage other public and private resources, employ unemployed neighborhood residents, save energy in the community, and build their internal capacity to the point that energy programs may even become self-supporting. They are successfully contributing to breaking the cycle of dependency on direct energy assistance payments.

Nonprofits are flexible enough that they can combine housing rehabilitation with energy assistance. Again, using Cleveland as an example, many local groups include furnace repair, storm windows, and insulation in the homes they rehabilitate.

As with foundations, nonprofits are deeply affected by federal policy changes and budget cuts. For example, the United Way of America's "Executive Newsletter" of June 1981 reported that one out of every five dollars cut from the federal budget would affect nonprofit organizations. They are constantly scrambling for new funding sources to replace government funds. Energy conservation programs can provide a source of income for nonprofits. As their expertise in this area grows, these programs can be used to provide job training to neighborhood residents and market the program to higher income households.

The independent sector's role in energy assistance for low-income households is very distinct from the public sector's role. The public sector must continue to provide the bulk of the funds, set minimum standards for service provision, and ensure some degree of program uniformity within and between states. The independent sector, on the other hand, plays an auxiliary role, bringing together public and private resources and enhancing public efforts at the local, community, or neighborhood level. Successful pilot projects initiated by the independent sector can be replicated and expanded by the public sector. For example, the Fitchburg (Massachusetts) Action to Conserve Energy began as a joint public/private effort funded, in part, through ACTION. It was replicated by ACTION in many other cities throughout the country. Many of the developments in alternative technology were initiated by community organizations.

In the face of cutbacks in federal programs, the private sector is being called upon to fill in the gaps. As the gaps widen to chasms, it becomes clearer that the private sector has neither the capacity nor the desire to become a major provider of social services. Richard Neblett, Exxon Corporation's manager of corporate contributions, was quoted in a *New York Times* article as saying, "It's important to remember that if you're going to cut $35 billion out of a budget, it's not going to be replaced by $3 billion (the level of corporate giving in 1983) from corporations."[6] Corporations are reluctant to fund government or ex-government programs through their foundations. Most use the basic rule of thumb that they pay taxes and that is as far as they will go to support government. Further, low-income energy assistance programs often do not meet the priorities set by corporate foundations, which prefer to fund education, culture, and arts programs.

A large portion of energy assistance policy involves the redistribution of income among different classes. This is outside the realm of the independent sector, which is better equipped to test new approaches and to provide the financing for nonprofits to carry out their energy assistance activities.

7

The Case For Utility Leadership

Utilities occupy a unique position in the overall energy picture. They straddle the public and private sector, fitting neatly into neither. Because of their unique economic and social position, both investor-owned and publicly owned utilities are regulated. A public utility—whether gas, electric, telephone, or water—provides an essential service to society that would be costly to duplicate.[1] Economically, utilities are considered "natural monopolies"—industries that, because of the massive capital investments required to deliver service, have large economies of scale. Regulation is required to provide adequate revenues and a fair rate of return to the company or stockholders so that the utility can continue to provide adequate service, and, at the same time, protect consumers from any unfair practices such as rate discrimination as well as to assure the service provided meets certain standards. Equity, efficiency and quality of service are the major objectives of utility regulation.[2]

Socially, utilities play a very important role. They are the major suppliers of our nation's heat, light, cooking fuel, telephone service, and water—all basic necessities in today's world. Utilities and their regulatory agencies have the unenviable role of balancing the concerns of economic efficiency and social equity, thus taking on both traditional private- and public–sector responsibilities. While this chapter focuses on the role of the energy utilities in this regard, Chapter 8 will focus on telephone companies.

For many years the attention of energy utility companies focused on the primary concern of economic efficiency. As long as they did not discriminate within customer class (that is, commercial, industrial, and residential), the social equity basically took care of itself. However, the energy crisis gave utility companies a new high level of visibility and, accordingly, social equity now has a more important role in utility decisions.

Susan M. Shanaman, chairman of the Pennsylvania Public Utility Commission, recognized this phenomenon. She said: "Regulators and utilities cannot escape the consequences of society's problems any more than they have been able to evade the efforts of prevailing economic conditions."[3]

Because of their unique position, the role of utilities in addressing these problems is under constant debate. While most parties to the debate would agree that utilities have an interest in assisting their low-income customers, there is little agreement on the appropriate course of action to be taken. Like the development of energy assistance policy in general, the utility sector's response to the low-income energy problem has been piecemeal, with a heavy reliance on trial and error.

For the most part, utilities themselves have done little to help define their role, preferring instead to react to commission orders, federal and state legislation, or consumer pressures in developing ways to deal with the problem. Those utilities that have taken an active role have done so for both economic efficiency and social equity concerns.

The utility's uncollectible accounts are directly affected by the problems faced by the poor and the elderly in paying their utility bills, especially when regulators impose shut-off moratoria during the winter months. This affects the company's "bottom line," creating a great deal of concern over inflation.

The problem of uncollectible accounts, as they are called, is universal, affecting all utility companies. It has encouraged both the gas and electric utilities to become strong advocates of federally and state–funded energy assistance programs, and, in the process, to become strong allies of national consumer advocacy groups on lobbying against threatened program cuts. Crises do, indeed, make strange bedfellows.

A second and much less universal economic consideration related to low-income energy assistance is conservation. Those utilities with rising fuel costs and short supplies view investments in conservation as a low-cost and reliable alternate source of energy. This is especially true of states with a rapidly growing population, high dependence on oil for generating power, or dependence on diminishing sources of water power.

Several utilities have taken their social responsibility seriously, if somewhat conservatively, and have ventured into energy assistance. This effort has been undertaken as part of their broader goal of maintaining a vital community in which to operate. The economic vitality of an individual utility is closely linked to the economic vitality of the area it serves. It cannot pack up its pipes (or take down its wires) and leave. These concerns led the American Gas Association and its member companies to adopt the position that "responsible actions are necessary to assist less fortunate customers in obtaining and paying for gas utility service. Such actions aid not only customers in need, but also help to maintain the economic vitality of the utilities and the communities they serve."[4]

Similarly the Edison Electric Institute urged its member companies to "engage in a full range of activities that will lessen the effect of escalating rates on the bill-paying burden of their customers, *especially those who are financially disadvantaged,* and will provide them with certain protections against the potential hardships of service disconnections."[5]

Surveys of member companies done by both the American Gas Association and the Edison Electric Institute reveal a broad range of utility involvement in energy assistance for the poor. As the shortfalls in government-sponsored programs grow, utilities can expect increased pressure from legislators, regulators, and consumers to take an even stronger role as assistance providers.

However, there are many, both within and outside the industry, who argue that energy assistance is a social problem that is best addressed by government. Utilities, it is believed, should not be tax collectors, subsidizing one income group at the expense of another, to finance programs. These critics argue that utility-sponsored assistance programs are inequitable and that financing them through the utility's rate base constitutes a regressive tax. Energy consumption, the argument goes, is a necessity and because the poor tend to use relatively large amounts of energy, they are "taxed" disproportionately by programs that recover costs through rates. Those who fall just above the income guidelines for assistance are hardest hit.

Even though most utilities offer some form of assistance to their low-income customers, the bulk of both program and funding initiatives still comes from the public sector. Utilities tend to become involved in five areas:

1. Consumer assistance—primarily information and referral to federal, state, and local assistance programs: "one-stop shopping" for assistance
2. Billing plans—that is, partial payment plans or budget billing
3. Expanded communications with elderly and low-income groups
4. Lobbying for federal, state, and local programs and funds
5. Information on energy conservation

However, several companies and state regulatory bodies have taken a more active role. They have successfully implemented fuel funds, offered energy conservation grants and loans, trained weatherization workers, and designed other innovative programs to address the low-income energy problem. (Lifeline and conservation rates, discussed in Chapter 4, are not included here because they were mandated by PURPA, and thus are not considered to be utility–initiated programs.)[6]

An examination of these innovative programs, their funding sources, and how they fit into the broader energy assistance picture offers insight to the different ways utilities have defined their role. Generally, these programs fall into three categories: (1) special billing and collection procedures, (2) direct assistance programs, and (3) conservation/weatherization programs.

BILL PAYMENTS AND COLLECTION PROCEDURES

The earliest action taken by utility companies in response to customers who were unable to pay their bills because of the sudden increase in prices was a relaxing of credit and termination policies. Many companies adopted one-third or one-sixth payment plans, which enabled customers to pay a portion of their bills to maintain service, particularly during the winter months. As the payment problems became more widespread, many state regulatory commissions adopted these policies and mandated them statewide; but even the one-sixth payment was beyond the budgets of many low-income families.

Restrictions on disconnection of service during cold weather months also became more common as regulators attempted to find an emergency solution to the problem. These moratoria became yearly events in many states and were usually accompanied by the requirement that customers enter into a repayment schedule, designed to bring their bills current before the next heating season. However, it soon became evident that the problem was not temporary but permanent and in fact became worse each year. The moratoria, minimum payment plans, and LIHEAP payments created a large number of "seasonal" utility customers. These customers were able to retain service during the winter months with the help of the programs but faced disconnection in the spring when assistance ended. Many states have adopted liberal enough reconnect policies that these customers can have service restored again in the late fall when the assistance programs go back into effect.[7] The moratoria are effective in preventing people from freezing in the winter but do nothing to resolve the problem that they are simply unable to pay. They continue to accumulate staggering arrearages with no prospects of repayment.

In an effort to address this snowball effect, a few states are experimenting with a new type of energy assistance program that involves utilities. Special payment programs have been enacted that enable low-income utility customers to pay a percentage of their monthly income to retain service. Such a program was implemented in Ohio in 1983. The Percentage–of–Income Payment Plan (PIP) enables customers to pay 10 percent of their income for their primary heating source and 5 percent for their secondary heating source during the winter months to retain service. During the summer months PIP customers pay their current bill or their PIP amount, whichever is higher, in an effort to catch up with arrearages accumulated during the winter. One problem with the program is that the issue of arrearages has not been adequately addressed. Some Ohio utilities count as much as $4 million in arrears on PIP accounts and the recovery mechanism is highly controversial.

This type of program adds a new dimension to direct assistance programs
by basing payments on income and subsidizing participants through an increase paid by all utility customers. Other states are watching the results of these programs carefully as they consider new ways to address the low-

income energy problem in light of the federal cutbacks in program funding.

DIRECT ASSISTANCE PROGRAMS

Other attempts to address the inability-to-pay issue are utility-supported or -sponsored bill-payment assistance funds or "fuel funds," as they are often called. These have been developed to provide a source of "last resort" assistance and have become increasingly popular as shortfalls in other forms of assistance became more evident. Fuel funds now exist in most states.

All fuel funds are based on a similar model: The utility provides seed money to start the fund, start-up administrative costs, and/or matches donations from customers, employees, stockholders, or the general public up to a maximum amount. Additional funds are often solicited from local businesses, charities, and in some cases government.

Some utilities fund the programs through corporate profit while others include them as operating expenses that can be recovered through rates. Still others use a combination of the two. One company, the Equitable Gas Company in Pittsburgh, funded its program through one-half of the profits realized from off-system sales of surplus gas to Eastern utilities for displacing fuel oil. In some cities, the gas, electric, and even water utilities contribute to a common fund.

Most utilities choose not to administer the funds directly, preferring to contract with a charitable organization like the Salvation Army or the American Red Cross. This keeps the utility at arm's length from actual distribution of funds.

The full impact of fuel funds is difficult to assess. However, a survey of credit managers of 60 gas and electric utilities done by the National Association of Credit Managers offers some idea of their scope. In 1984–85, at least $8 million was spent by utility companies to support fuel funds in at least 39 states. Company dollars to support these funds ranged from a low of $20,000 to a high of $800,000, with the average company spending about $250,000. Benefits paid to needy customers ranged from $35 to $500, with most companies limiting the amount to $200.[8]

In almost every case, the utilities solicit additional funds from customers, other corporations, stockholders, or the general public to support their fuel funds. While at first glance it might seem that these funds would contribute to reducing the utilities' uncollectibles, in fact, the survey found the funds had minimal or no impact on utility collection statistics. Rather, the greatest benefit of these funds to the utilities, according to the survey, was in the positive public relations generated by the programs—people perceived that the utilities were doing "something" about the low-income energy problem.

Utilities established fuel funds for a number of reasons. Some responded to pressure from consumer advocates or local governments. Others saw it as a way to provide last–resort assistance to those who had exhausted all other sources and fell through the gaps in state and federal programs. Whatever their reasons, a growing number of utilities are implementing fuel funds. Despite their growing numbers, however, these programs are stopgap, preventing or postponing disconnection of service only temporarily.

CONSERVATION/WEATHERIZATION PROGRAMS

The federal Residential Conservation Service program, enacted in 1978, mandated that states adopt plans requiring regulated utility companies to offer home energy audits to their customers. As a result RCS audits are now available in most (not all) states.

The significance of the RCS program for low-income energy assistance lies in its mandate to states to get utility companies involved in conservation, at least at a very basic level. Beyond that, it is the states' prerogative to carry conservation further.

Some states took the federal mandate seriously and required utilities to go far beyond the audits. However, most states set guidelines and then left the programs to the utility companies, which were often less than enthusiastic in implementing them.

At best, RCS is used by utilities as a marketing tool for conservation. By providing homeowners with the dollars and cents of energy savings specific to their own homes, the audit provides the incentive for further investments in conservation. At worst, RCS is seen by utilities as another regulation to be complied with in letter but not in spirit. Participation rates nationwide are low, ranging from .5 to 3 percent, and one-half of all audited customers fail to make any conservation improvements.[9]

While RCS was not designed specifically to serve low-income people, it does have the potential of reaching this group. However, nationwide, low-income utility customers participated at a rate of less than one-half the rate for other income groups.[10] Some localities were able to achieve a higher rate of low-income participation through specially designed RCS programs. These were developed by individual utilities, often in response to pressure from low-income energy assistance advocates.

For example, in Cleveland the East Ohio Gas (EOG) Company agreed to contract with a broad–based neighborhood development organization to do the RCS audits in low- and moderate–income neighborhoods. This organization agreed to subcontract with neighborhood groups to do the audits, using an audit instrument designed specifically for the older housing stock common in Cleveland's low- and moderate–income neighborhoods.

Linking the RCS audits with local housing groups makes the audits accessible to low- and moderate–income households. It gives the auditors, who work for the groups and in most cases are neighborhood residents, greater credibility, and it links RCS with a variety of housing rehabilitation and energy conservation grant and loan programs sponsored by the state, the city, local corporations, and foundations.

After 22 months in operation, the Neighborhood Energy Audit Program exceeded its original goals. Over 57 percent of all EOG audits completed in the Cleveland area were done through the program.

The audits are used as a marketing tool for energy conservation by neighborhood groups. Homes are being weatherized at a rate of 1,400 per year, which translates into $2.2 million per year in weatherization work. In addition, the program employs 25 full- or part-time auditors, 4 audit coordinators, and 2 audit processors.

Based on the program's success, it has been expanded within EOG's service area. Three Akron groups now subcontract to do the audits. They have completed 600 audits since fall 1984, one-third of all audits done in Akron since 1981. The state of Ohio has committed about $300,000 to replicate Cleveland's program statewide in conjunction with a low-interest loan program for conservation, the Ohio Energy Action Program.

EOG's Neighborhood Energy Audit program has audited 6,912 homes and encouraged an annual investment of about $2.2 million in energy conservation in target neighborhoods. It has created 18 full-time jobs and a new income source for neighborhood development groups amounting to almost $8,000 a month. Overall, the program has had a very positive economic impact on low- and moderate–income neighborhoods in EOG's service area.

Other utility conservation and weatherization programs are usually mandated by state regulators, often in response to state legislation. Thus, utility involvement in conservation/weatherization depends in large part on the state's political and regulatory climate and its commitment to conservation. States with a strong conservation ethic such as Florida, California, Oregon, Washington, Michigan, and Minnesota carried the RCS mandate beyond the audits. In fact, they had energy conservation financing programs in place prior to RCS and used RCS as an opportunity to expand their programs further. These states regard conserved energy as a new, lower-cost alternative to traditional supplies. Both gas and electric utilities in these states are required to invest in conservation in an effort to increase supply and decrease cost.

For example, the Pacific Northwest has traditionally relied on once-plentiful hydro power to generate electricity. Because of its relatively low cost, many households used it as their primary heating fuel. As a new growth phase began to outstrip the generating capacity of the existing plants, utilities were faced with the prospect of either reducing demand through conservation or building new expensive and unpopular nuclear–powered generators. They chose conservation as a load management technique.

The economics that led public utility regulatory bodies and public utilities in many states to invest in conservation are extremely complex. They are based on the premise that these investments make economic sense for the utility companies which are beginning to see their function as energy management rather than energy sales. From the perspective of public utility commissions and companies, investments in conservation are viewed as less expensive, in the long run, than investments in new plant and equipment or, in the case of gas utilities, the purchase of new higher priced sources of gas.

For example, the Michigan Public Service Commission initiated its Home Insulation Promotion and Financing Program in 1973, which required Michigan's utilities to develop conservation programs. The Commission had a relatively long history of involvement with energy conservation, consistent with its concern for the effects of rising utility costs on customers, particularly those with low incomes. A projection of continued natural gas shortages (which proved inaccurate), a lack of insulation in Michigan's homes, rising energy prices, and the expense of developing and producing alternative sources of gas prompted William G. Rosenberg, then Commission chairman, to initiate this program. The program was expanded in 1976 to include interest-free loans for conservation measures with a seven-year payback and furnace retrofits. The cost of these loans is considered part of the utilities' rate base. As an incentive to participate in this program, utilities are permitted a higher return on capital invested in conservation. Costs are actually recovered through a uniform surcharge per unit of gas or electricity consumed by all customer classes.

Perhaps the most significant aspect of Michigan's program in terms of promoting conservation is its coordination with the state's RCS program. The Commission has taken the federal mandate to develop an RCS plan as an opportunity to blend state and federal programs. Michigan's RCS is used as an umbrella to coordinate energy audits and utility financing of insulation.

Another economic argument in favor of investing in conservation is illustrated by the Massachusetts Department of Public Utilities' "no losses test." Based on marginal cost pricing, the test requires that the cost of saving KWH be less than or equal to the marginal cost of new generation, transmission, or distribution capacity, if it is needed. However, it is difficult to identify accurately the value of long-term savings, especially in states currently experiencing an energy supply glut. Within the conservation-oriented states, however, the quality, effectiveness, and creativity of the programs vary depending on the individual utility's commitment to conservation.

In examining utility-financed conservation programs, the relevant question is the extent to which these benefit low-income customers. Those programs that offer loans, at market rate or below, generally exclude the low-income. Interest–free loans may be slightly more accessible but grants, cash rebates, or in-kind assistance best meet the needs of low-income households. California, Michigan, and Oregon have excellent track records in insulating the homes of low-income residents. They require that the weatherization measures installed be cost-effective, usually over a five- to seven-year period. (Southern California Gas Company has weatherized 30,000 homes at no cost to the homeowner. Michigan has insulated over 3,000 ceilings through its utility program.)

Some utilities have taken the initiative and developed conservation programs even without a state mandate. For example, Baltimore Gas and Electric Company (BG&E) committed over $200,000 a year, beginning in 1981, to the Baltimore Energy Alliance Program, a joint project with the state and city of Baltimore. It provides free weatherization and conservation education to low-income homeowners. As of April 1984 the program had weatherized 3,385 homes. In 1982 the program was expanded to include rented property and has weatherized 545 units. BG&E also has an elderly loan program to finance energy-related repairs and improvements. Loans have seven–year terms and 11.5 percent interest rates.

An increasingly popular utility program for low-income customers is no-cost/low-cost conservation. These programs are designed to encourage customers to do-it-themselves. Caulking, weatherstripping, plastic storm windows, faucet flow restrictors, and other do-it-yourself materials are provided. Several utilities offer these kits to low-income families in conjunction with their audit programs. Others hold workshops or distribute them on a broad scale to interested customers. Still others have donated these kits to nonprofit community organizations that then hire and train neighborhood youth or unemployed workers to install them directly in people's homes, most often those of senior citizens and LIHEAP recipients. For example, Alabama Gas Company recently installed caulking, plastic windows, and door sweeps in 15,000 homes of their low-income customers (LIHEAP recipients). The company employed 350 low-income and unemployed teens for the summer to install these air inflation barriers. This pilot program was such a success that the company plans to repeat it again. Total program cost was $1.5 million. These kits serve as as first step in stopping air infiltration to the home. Those programs that are most successful include an educational component and are accompanied by a workshop or a one-on-one demonstration by an auditor or a neighborhood worker and a follow-up visit to assure proper usage. They alert people to the areas of heat loss in their homes and get them thinking along the lines of conservation. They offer utilities high visibility at a relatively low cost.

Utilities are also involved in conservation through their corporate donations programs. In-kind or cash donations for trucks, insulation-blowing machines, and materials help to support nonprofit conservation programs.

An example of a public-private weatherization financing program is the Energy Bank administered by Minnegasco. It is capitalized by $3 million in tax-exempt revenue bonds issued by the Minneapolis Community Development Agency. The bank offers below-market-interest-rate loans (11 percent) to any Minneapolis resident. To gain access to the energy bank, residents must first have an audit done either through a city program of neighborhood energy workshops or the utility's RCS program. This unique public-private program could also be structured to offer loans to investor-owned multifamily buildings, but the high interest rate precludes low-income households from participating.

More recently, utilities have become involved in low-interest loan guarantees for the purchase of efficient natural gas furnaces and the retrofit of existing furnaces. These measures can be very cost-effective.

Utilities can also play a role in educating customers about the benefits of energy conservation. Money is often not the only barrier to undertaking conservation efforts. Many households do not understand that energy costs can be controlled and that savings (or at least costs avoided) are possible.

To educate its customers, Northern States Power Company in Minneapolis/St. Paul purchased and renovated a 100-year-old home in a transitional low/moderate-income neighborhood in Minneapolis and a second home in St. Paul for use as energy-learning centers. The centers are designed to demonstrate the feasibility of weatherizing existing structures. They offer "hands on" conservation/weatherization information.

Other companies rely on their speakers' bureaus or consumer affairs departments to educate customers. Many offer educational materials to schools to promote understanding of conservation concepts and techniques.

Utility involvement in energy assistance is becoming more significant as the original players—federal, state, and local government—reassess their roles. Utilities are becoming more attuned to the concerns of their customers and many have established consumer advisory boards to guide them through difficult decisions regarding their low-income customers. Through these and other mutual consciousness-raising efforts utilities better define the relationship between their social equity responsibilities and their economic efficiency responsibilities. The de-emphasis on federal assistance, coupled with a more aggressive state regulatory climate, will result in more utility programs that benefit low-income customers in the areas of both direct assistance and conservation, either by choice or by mandate. A challenge for regulators and legislators will be to examine current regulatory policies and practices as well as federal and state laws to remove barriers to this trend and provide further incentives for utility company leadership.

PART IV

A NEW CRISIS/A NEW APPROACH

8

Telephone Rates and the Poor

INTRODUCTION: TELEPHONE AND ENERGY RATES

The preceding chapters have traced the responses of government agencies, public utilities, and other organizations to the dramatic increase in energy rates and the resulting impact on low-income consumers.

For over a decade, policies have been debated and programs enacted that have sought to assure adequate energy supplies for those households that cannot afford them. Because the energy issue was thrust upon us in such a dramatic fashion with the oil embargo of 1973, and since the initial policy responses focused almost exclusively on assuring adequate supplies of energy, it was not until the late 1970s that federal and state policy makers began coming to grips with the inevitable impact of the price increases. While the problem has not been solved and in many cases it has been exacerbated by diminished federal funding support during the Reagan administration, many innovative programs, developed at the state and local levels, have now begun to address the plight of the low-income and fixed-income energy consumer.

A basic premise of this book is that there is much to be learned in looking back over this decade of policy and program development that can be useful as public- and private-sector officials confront the current and projected increases in the cost of another basic utility: local telephone service. If the decade of the 1970s was characterized as the years of "the energy crisis," ten years from now, the 1980s decade may well be characterized as the years of "the telephone crisis."

The divestiture of the American Telephone and Telegraph Company (AT&T) and regulatory decisions by the Federal Communications Commission (FCC) have led to increasing pressures on local telephone companies and state regulatory commissions to significantly raise local telephone service rates. What can we draw from the experience of this past decade to assure that local telephone service, which literally is a "lifeline" for many, will be maintained?

While the average electric bill increased by 179 percent and natural gas bills went up 367 percent from 1973–83, telephone bills increased only 64 percent. This latter increase was below the inflationary trend that plagued the U.S. economy during that same period, as illustrated in Figure 8.1. With telephone rates remaining relatively low during this period, the concept of "universal service" has not been threatened.

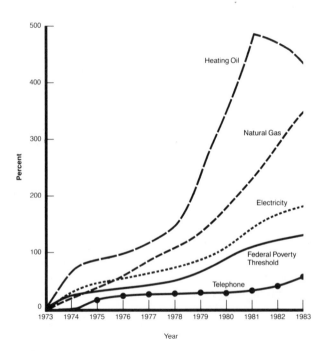

Figure 8.1
Percent Increase in Energy Prices and Federal Poverty Threshold, 1973-83

Sources: (for natural gas, electricity and telephone, 1974-81), reprinted from *The Politics of Public Utility Regulation* by William T. Gormley, Jr., by permission of the University of Pittsburgh Press, © 1983 by the University of Pittsburgh Press; (1981-83) U.S. Department of Energy, Energy Information Administration, *State Energy Price and Expenditures Report, 1984,* (Washington, D.C., December 1984), p. 6; (federal poverty threshold) U.S. Department of Commerce, Bureau of the Census, *Statistical Abstract of the United States, 1984* (Washington, D.C., December 1983), p. 471; (telephone) National Association of Regulatory Utility Commissioners, derived from monthly rates for residential customers purchasing one-party flat rate service; (heating oil) Diane DeVaul, "Narrowing the Gap—The Energy Needs of the Poor and Federal Funding," Issue Brief, (Washington, D.C.: Northeast-Midwest Institute, April 30, 1987), p. 2. Reprinted with permission.

A NATIONAL POLICY OF UNIVERSAL SERVICE

The term "universal service" appears in no public law. It was first used by Theodore Vail, the architect and guiding force of the AT&T system in the late 1800s and early 1900s. Vail's motto was: one system, one policy, universal service. Title I of The Communications Act of 1934, the cornerstone of federal telecommunications policy, establishes a national objective: "to make available, so far as possible, to all the people of the United States a rapid, efficient, nationwide and worldwide wire and radio communication service with adequate facilities at reasonable charges."[1]

Stated or not in the law, the concept of universal service, if measured by the percent of households with telephone service, is a concept that gained widespread support and a national policy objective that has been essentially achieved. The trends over the past several decades in attaining universal telephone service are shown in Table 8.1. While it is possible to argue what exactly is meant by universal service, it is clear that telephone service is avail-

Table 8.1
Development of U.S. Telephone Service

Year	Telephones per 100 People[1]	Percent of All Households with Telephone Service[2]	Percent with Dial Service[2]
1900	2		
1910	8		
1920	13		
1930	16		
1940	17		
1945	21	46	58
1950	28	62	71
1955	34	72	84
1960	41	79	96
1965	48	85	100
1970	59	91	100
1975	69	94	100
1980	79	96	100

Source: [1]Federal Communications Commission, *Statistics of Communications Common Carriers; Statistical Abstract of the United States,* as cited in U.S., Congress, Congressional Budget Office, *The Changing Telephone Industry: Access Charges, Universal Service, and Local Rates,* study prepared for Senator Barry Goldwater, chairman of the Communications Subcommittee of the Senate Committee on Commerce, Science and Transportation, by Peyton L. Wynns, June 1984, p. 56, Table B-1. Reprinted with permission.

Source: [2]*Bell System Statistical Manuals,* 1973 and 1982 editions, as cited in U.S., Congress, Congressional Budget Office, *The Changing Telephone Industry: Access Charges, Universal Service, and Local Rates,* study prepared for Senator Barry Goldwater, chairman of the Communications Subcommittee of the Senate Committee on Commerce, Science and Transportation, by Peyton L. Wynns, June 1984, p. 58, Table B-2. Reprinted with permission.

able in well over 90 percent of the households in the United States. As was illustrated in response to the low-income energy issue, these customers can become a major political force if this concept of universal service is threatened.

THREATS TO THE POLICY

The "threats" to universal service emerge from a number of recent court and regulatory actions related to the telecommunications industry. First and foremost is the 1982 federal–court–approved settlement of the U.S. Department of Justice antitrust suit against AT&T whereby the company agreed to divest the local Bell operating companies, which accounted for more than half of the corporation's assets. At the same time, AT&T was freed of the restriction against entering various computer- and information–related service markets.

This court action, when combined with decisions of the FCC initiating access charges for residential and business customers of local telephone companies and changing the required depreciation methodologies used in establishing telephone service rates, has led to dramatically increasing charges for basic telephone service. Telephone company officials and many telecommunication policy experts also have argued for addressing the regulatory constraints, such as depreciation methodologies that retard the ability of a company to incorporate rapidly changing technologies in the telecommunications industry. And, more recently, serious proposals have been put forth for full deregulation of the telephone industry.

While the debate continues on the long-term impacts of divestiture and the FCC policy and decisions seeking to enhance the competitive environment in telecommunications, the reality is that local telephone rates are increasing substantially. Some households will not be able to afford to pay and will lose service. The challenge for state regulators, legislators, telephone utility executives, and consumers' groups is to address this inevitable consequence before it also becomes a reality.

To illustrate, in 1983 there were $7 billion to $9 billion worth of telephone rate increases under consideration before state public utility commissioners and the media was reporting that the average customer's bill of $11.91 was projected to rise to $30 to $35 in Texas and Tennessee and possibly increasing to above $200 a month in rural Alaskan communities. While the policy debate surrounding divestiture began to develop in earnest, the Cleveland *Plain Dealer* summarized current concerns by stating in an editorial of July 24, 1983, "Telephones are not luxuries. They are rights ... " Although telephone bills have lagged behind inflation rates in the past decade, local service rates will exceed inflation rates in the future. Susan W. Leisner, commissioner of the Florida Public Service Commission, stated: "Inflation is now hovering at around 4 percent while rate requests are reflecting 50 percent to 250 percent increases."[2] Having absorbed energy price increases at above-inflation rates for a decade, the poor are now confronted with a similar future for telephone charges.

In 1983 the National Governors' Association (NGA) established a Universal Telephone Service Task Force, which had a twofold mission: "First, to sensitize officials and the public to the impact of the FCC and AT&T court decision. Second, to attempt to influence Congress to act quickly in a positive manner to resolve the threat to universal telephone service."[3] The NGA identified key actions that were the source of the threat to universal service (see Table 8.2).

In testimony before the NGA Task Force, William A. Spratley, Consumer Counsel for the State of Ohio, stated: "Federal regulatory and court decisions threaten to double monthly telephone bills. . . . I want to stress why 'lifeline' telephone rates must be fashioned by state public utility commissioners in the face of the new 'federal price tag' on local telephone bills."[4]

Related testimony provided in 1983 by Eric J. Schneidewind, chairman of the Michigan Public Service Commission says:

It is quite likely that many states will see a tripling of basic telephone service costs rather than a doubling, and in these states it is quite possible that one out of every four customers could lose basic telephone service. It is my conclusion that a loss of basic service in the magnitude described above will destroy the concept of universal telephone service in this country.[5]

In supporting his estimates Schneidewind cited FCC studies on price elasticities and stated: "In other words, the FCC conclusion is that a price in-

Table 8.2
Threats to Universal Service in 1984:
The Source of the Problem

	Estimated % Increase on Local Rates
Actions by the FCC	
Charges for consumer access to long-distance network	39%
Preemption of intrastate depreciation rate setting for local telephone companies	25%
Deregulation of telephone equipment (CPE)	16%
Preemption of accounting treatment for inside wire	6%
Effect of Divestiture on Bell Operating Co. Profitability	
Loss of intrastate toll revenue, cost of reconfiguring the network to meet equal access requirements, restrictions on BOCs to provide only basic service, contingent anti-trust liabilities, transactional costs	84%
Other: Inflation, Wage Increases, Etc.	20%
Total 1984 Estimated Increase	**190%**

Source: The National Governors' Association, August 1983. Reprinted with permission.

crease for basic telephone service customers of 100 percent will cause 10 percent of these customers to drop their basic telephone service."

The NGA Task Force reviewed data that demonstrated the projected threat to universal service. While basic telephone service is available in over 90 percent of U.S. households, the impact of anticipated telephone rate increases would fall most heavily on the young, black, and rural households. This projected impact is shown in Table 8.3.

Just as there is no widely agreed upon or exact definition of universal service, it is equally difficult to define when a threat to universal service becomes a reality. To paraphrase U.S. Supreme Court Justice Potter Stewart, who spoke candidly in another policy and legal debate, "I don't know how to define it, but I know it when I see it."[6] Certainly if service levels were to drop below one-third of major demographic categories, as projected by the NGA Task Force, we no longer would have a recognizable policy of universal service.

THE RESPONSE TO THE THREATS

Unlike the policy debates on energy assistance for low-income households that were slow in getting started after the 1973 oil embargo, the same

Table 8.3
Estimated Percentage of Households with Basic Telephone Service

Demographic Characteristics	Price Increase			
	Base	50%	100%	200%
All	91.52	88.15	83.59	70.92
Young	85.39	80.12	73.54	56.92
Black	86.37	81.38	75.08	58.89
Rural	88.84	84.59	79.10	64.38
Moderately Poor	83.81	78.12	71.11	53.93
Young	72.18	64.14	55.22	36.97
Black	75.25	67.71	59.12	40.74
Rural	79.26	72.48	64.50	46.34
Very Poor	79.28	72.48	64.53	46.38
Young	64.99	56.14	46.88	29.56
Black	69.21	60.78	51.66	33.69
Rural	73.85	66.07	57.31	38.96

Source: (for household demographic and economic data) U.S., Department of Commerce, Bureau of the Census, *Money Income of Households in the United States: 1979* and *Household and Family Characteristics: March 1980* (Washington, D.C.: U.S. Government Printing Office); (for telephone rate information) American Telephone and Telegraph Company, Market and Service Plans Department, Research Section, Market Research Information Systems (MRIS). Reprinted with permission.

has not been true in seeking to confront the anticipated significant increase in telephone rates for local service customers. Congressional and state legislative hearings, consumer and telephone company proposals, and state and federal regulatory actions were all well under way throughout the country prior to the final implementation of AT&T divestiture, which became effective January 1, 1984. In many jurisdictions the debate continues while in a few cases, mostly at the state level, programs have been put in place.

As has been done in tracing the response to the energy assistance issue, the following discussion provides an overview of the initial public- and private-sector response. As was true with the energy issue, initial debate has focused on rates and "disconnect" issues.

The Federal Response

As the AT&T case was concluding and the steps for implementing divestiture were being taken, a number of bills were introduced into the U.S. Congress to ameliorate the anticipated impact of these pending actions, reverse or delay some of the proposed additional charges on local service customers, and in general preserve the concept of universal service. In testifying in support of the Universal Telephone Preservation Act of 1983, Edward Hipp, a commissioner of the North Carolina Public Utilities Commission and chairman of NARUC's (National Association of Regulatory Utility Commissioners) Communication Committee, stated:

The primary reason [for supporting the legislation] is the turmoil that we see coming in telecommunication regulation, which will come close to being a crisis if it goes on without any abatement or without any change, because we feel that the burdens being placed upon a substantial number of users by the rate increases threatened by the deregulation changes will be too great.[7]

The primary purpose as stated in the legislation was "to assure the availability to all the people of the United States affordable, reliable, efficient communication services which are essential to full participation in the Nation's economic, political and social life."[8] The hearings on the legislation documented the concerns of many state regulators that anticipated rate increases would disproportionately fall on low-income households. Emerging from these hearings was a report stating:

The Congress finds that: significant rate increases will threaten universal service by forcing many Americans, especially the poor, the elderly, the handicapped, and those living in high cost urban and rural areas to discontinue their telephone service; and the national interest demands that telephone service continues to be universally available at affordable rates.[9]

As the NGA Task Force discussion illustrates, there are numerous factors involved in the projected telephone rate increases; however, much of the congressional debate has focused on the access charge issue. For example, in hearings on the Universal Telephone Preservation Act of 1983, Congressman John Dingle, chairman of the U.S. House of Representatives Committee on Energy and Commerce, read into the record Judge Green's views on the access charge decision:

This decision undermines one of the assumptions underlying the court's approval of the decree, that there be no impairment of the principle of universal service . . . ninety-one percent of all households now have telephones. As the FCC's access fee reaches $7 as it will in a few years, this is estimated to drop to 60 percent for very poor blacks, 65 percent for very poor living in rural areas, and 58 percent for poor young couples.[10]

In questioning FCC Chairman Mark S. Fowler, Chairman Dingle raised this issue:

It is the Congress's policy that we shall have universal service, which means that we shall have telephone and telecommunications service as widely available as possible. Isn't this FCC decision going to cause a significant disruption of the number of telephones and the amount of service available to large groups within our society, principally the very poor, those in rural areas? Chairman Fowler's response: We do not know that sir.[11]

The postdivestiture environment has been clouded with many debates between experts and confusion among consumers related to just why and how much rates actually will increase. The issue at the heart of the congressional debate relates to the FCC's order that establishes "access charges" paid by each telephone subscriber. These charges have been devised as a means for the local telephone companies to recover their fixed costs. Since local telephone company facilities are used both to complete local calls and long distance calls, a share of the local fixed costs historically has been recovered from long distance revenues.

Over the past 30 years there has been a significant increase in the costs allocated against interstate service as illustrated in Figure 8.2. This allocation far exceeds the long distance usage in contrast to local service usage. The wide variation in allocation of these costs in the states is shown in Table 8.4, which indicates the U.S. average interstate cost allocation was 26 percent, but the range was from 13 percent to 62 percent. As concluded by the Congressional Budget Office,

the use of access charges to recover local fixed costs will align long-distance rates more closely with the costs of providing that service and reduce incentives for high volume telecommunication users to develop private systems that do not share the

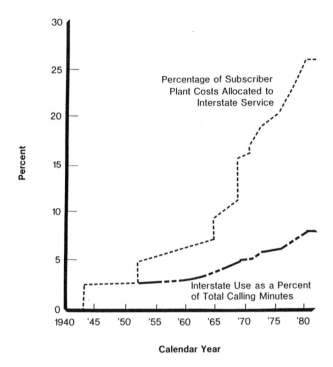

Figure 8.2
Percentage of Subscriber Plant Costs Allocated to Interstate Service

Source: AT&T data, as cited in U.S., Congress, Congressional Budget Office, *The Changing Telephone Industry: Access Charges, Universal Service, and Local Rates,* study prepared for Senator Barry Goldwater, chairman of the Communications Subcommittee of the Senate Committee on Commerce, Science and Transportation, by Peyton L. Wynns, June 1984, p. 10, Figure 1. Reprinted with permission.

fixed cost paid by other users. At the same time, however, access charges will impose higher fixed monthly charges on subscribers.[12]

While the initial congressional debate focused primarily on the access charge issue, since it is most amenable to congressional action, proposals also were considered to preserve universal service also call for the establishment of "lifeline" telephone service.

Bills were introduced in both the 98th and 99th Congresses (1984 and 1985) and FCC actions have sought to address these issues. The Universal Telephone Preservation Act of 1983 (HR 4102) passed the House in November 1983. It prohibited the FCC from imposing the access charge approach to cost allocation and would continue the utilization of long distance tolls to partially underwrite local service. The Senate version (S 1660) called for a moratorium on the access charge until January 1, 1986. The Senate bill

Table 8.4

Bell System Subscriber Plant Costs for 1981 and Interstate
Allocation of Subscriber Plant Costs per Subscriber Line
per Month

Local Bell Company	Subscriber Plant Costs (In Dollars)	Percentage Allocated to Interstate (SPF)	Amount Allocated to Interstate (In Dollars)
Alabama	32	20.8	7
Arizona	28	42.6	12
Arkansas	33	28.8	9
California	27	24.0	6
Colorado	30	42.2	13
Connecticut	23	33.4	8
Delaware	24	34.0	8
District of Columbia	23	41.9	10
Florida	35	36.2	13
Georgia	31	28.5	9
Idaho-Mountain Bell	27	35.3	9
Idaho-Pacific Northwest Bell	28	37.8	11
Illinois	22	26.4	6
Indiana	24	23.1	6
Iowa	25	28.2	7
Kansas	27	29.8	8
Kentucky-South Central Bell	32	20.3	7
Kentucky-Cincinnati Bell	22	13.0	3
Louisiana	34	19.9	7
Maine	25	29.9	7
Maryland	23	21.1	5
Massachusetts	23	27.5	6
Michigan	24	16.9	4
Minnesota	25	26.6	7
Mississippi	36	25.0	9
Missouri	25	26.3	7
Montana	27	44.5	12
Nebraska	27	36.9	10
Nevada	42	62.1	26
New Hampshire	28	43.0	12
New Jersey	22	31.5	7
New Mexico	27	36.0	10
New York	27	27.4	7
North Carolina	28	24.1	7
North Dakota	30	32.4	10
Ohio-Ohio Bell	23	19.0	4
Ohio-Cincinnati	23	18.7	4
Oklahoma	26	31.8	8
Oregon	27	32.8	9
Pennsylvania	20	21.1	4
Rhode Island	22	28.4	6
South Carolina	32	22.0	7
South Dakota	28	36.2	10
Tennessee	27	22.2	6

Table 8.4
(Continued)

Local Bell Company	Subscriber Plant Costs (In Dollars)	Percentage Allocated to Interstate (SPF)	Amount Allocated to Interstate (In Dollars)
Texas-Southwestern Bell	30	22.6	7
Utah	24	31.4	8
Vermont	29	43.9	13
Virginia	26	26.7	7
Washington	24	30.1	7
West Virginia	32	21.5	7
Wisconsin	21	21.7	5
Wyoming	45	56.5	5
System Average	26	26.0	7

Source: Federal Communications Commission, Common Carrier Docket No. 78-72, Phase 1; Comments of the Bell Operating Companies, 6 August 1982, as cited in U.S., Congress, Congressional Budget Office, *The Changing Telephone Industry: Access Charges, Universal Service, and Local Rates,* study prepared for Senator Barry Goldwater, chairman of the Communications Subcommittee of the Senate Committee on Commerce, Science and Transportation, by Peyton L. Wynns, June 1984, pp. 12-13, Table 3. Reprinted with permission.

was tabled and the Congress adjourned without specific action. During the debate the FCC postponed full implementation of the access charge approach and has subsequently put in place the following schedule: 1985 = $1, 1986 = $2, 1987 = $2.60, 1988 = $3.20, and 1989 = $3.50.

While differing on the access issue, both House and Senate legislation called for a reduced rate on lifeline service. In fact, in the 99th Congress legislation specifically entitled "The Lifeline Telephone Service Act of 1985" was introduced. While the Congress has yet to enact formal legislation, the lifeline issue continues to be the subject of legislative, regulatory and consumer debate.

Lifeline Telephone Service

In the 1970s lifeline service was a major initial policy response to rising energy rates.[13] With telephone service, the congressional proposals stated:

Lifeline telephone service is defined as basic telephone service intended to include a limited number of outgoing telephone calls in the local exchange area, with a per-call charge for any additional calls. Lifeline service is available to only primary residences with a single telephone line. Lifeline service, however, may not include what is now commonly referred to as measured, budget or economy service, where telephone service charges are based on the number, distance and duration of time spent on telephone calls. The charge for lifeline telephone service cannot be less than 33 percent, nor more than 50 percent, of the average charge for residential telephone exchange service in the exchange area.[14]

State public utility commissioners would be required to define the specific lifeline service. The target population that would be eligible for the service was also left to the states.

All telephone companies that instituted the service would be eligible for partial reimbursement payments from a fund, referred to as the Universal Service Fund or the Lifeline Service Fund, to offset the cost of providing the service. Payment levels would be based on partial payment (50 percent) of the difference between the lifeline rate and the average charge for residential service in the service area. The fund would be established using a surcharge on interstate long-distance tolls. The remainder of the unrecovered costs associated with the lifeline service would be made up from other telephone company services. The Congressional Budget Office estimates the costs to support lifeline service would be $680 million annually assuming participation by 11.3 million households.[15] Table 8.5 summarizes the initial proposals at the federal level for the telephone rates and the poor issue.

The State Response

Governors, state public utility commissioners, and state legislators in all states have expressed concerns regarding federal actions and their impact on local telephone service. State officials in testimony before the Congress have advocated a variety of responses to the telephone rate issue.

In 1983 the NARUC Communications Committee identified the principles (summarized below) relating to federal actions for which there was general support at the state level:

1. Overturn FCC access charge decisions and give state commissions the flexibility to set access charges under uniform national guidelines with FCC review.

2. Require interstate carriers, including bypassers, to pay access charges or surcharges for the use and upkeep of the local exchange.

3. Provide for an orderly transition from the present system of jurisdictional separations to an access charge structure.

4. Require state commissions to generate sufficient funds within each state to preserve universal service.

5. Provide limited interstate revenue sharing for exchange carriers if a state cannot internally generate sufficient revenue without jeopardizing universal service.

6. Create a Universal Service Board consisting of five federal and four state

Table 8.5
Lifeline Telephone Service: Initial Federal Proposals

Component	Original FCC Decision[1] 12/22/82	H.R. 4102[1] 1983	S. 1660[1] 1983
Lifeline service availability	States may require	Mandatory for all states	States may require
Subscriber access charges for lifeline subscribers	FCC may waive access charges	N/A residential access charges prohibited	No provision
Costs of lifeline service not paid by subscribers will be paid from	Other service offerings	50% from Universal Service Fund; 50% from other service offerings	Up to 50% from U.S.F.; remainder from O.S.O.
Funding for subsidy will come from	Universal Service Fund	Universal Service Fund	Universal Service Fund
Estimated size of fund	$900 million	$554 million	$180 million
Final decisions on changes in allocation and recovery made by	FCC	New Universal Service Board	New Universal Service Board (Joint)
Eligibility criteria for exchange common carriers to be compensated	All co. having average cost > 115% on nat'l average	Small co. w/costs > 110% of nat'l avg.; large co. w/costs 150%	Small co. receiving REA loans and having costs higher than 110% nat'l average

Source: [1]U.S., Congress, Congressional Budget Office, *The Changing Telephone Industry: Access Charges, Universal Service, and Local Rates,* study prepared for Senator Barry Goldwater, chairman of the Communications Subcommittee of the Senate Committee on Commerce, Science and Transportation, by Peyton L. Wynns, June 1984, pp. 36-37, Table 5.

members for the purpose of establishing uniform nationwide procedures and administering a universal service fund.

7. Retain state commission authority to describe methods by which exchange carriers recover investment and promote economic viability and recover the investment over its useful service life. (Reverse preemption of depreciation methods.)

8. Allow state commissions to make available a basic telephone instrument from the exchange carriers on a fully compensatory basis.

9. Permit state commissions to establish basic lifeline telephone rates designed to encourage universal service.

10. Permit cross-subsidization between regulated telecommunications services and unregulated commercial activities of carriers.

11. Permit state commissions to designate one or more interexchange carriers of last resort within each state.
12. Preserve 911 as a nationwide access number.

Surveys undertaken in 1984 and 1985 by NARUC and Cleveland State University's College of Urban Affairs documented the significant level of discussion in the states and the variety of approaches being considered. While discussions were widespread, by 1984 only California and Arkansas had implemented a targeted lifeline telephone rate. Some officials considered the more widely available options of budget or measured service, with increased or limited call allowances as responses to the low-income telephone users' needs. Pragmatically, they may be correct, for these budget services accomplish what many lifeline proposals call for: lower rates. But the budget services are not targeted for any special class of customer.

While specific proposals were being considered by state legislatures or public utility commissions, the surveys also indicate that nearly one-fifth of the states currently have legislative or constitutional prohibitions against approving targeted lifeline rates. Also, the states responding were overwhelmingly opposed to the federal lifeline legislation under consideration. This characterized a strong inclination on the part of state officials to develop their own response to the challenge of telephone rate increases. The surveys' results are summarized in Table 8.6. Several states have taken the lead in responding to the lifeline issue and the specific efforts of California and Arkansas are described to illustrate this initial programmatic response.

The California Response

The State of California was first to respond with a universal lifeline telephone service proposal: The rate is targeted for low-income households with $11,000 or less annual income, elderly, and handicapped. Each year the eligible households must self-certify to the local telephone company to receive a 50 percent reduction in the available residential rate and associated charges. The components of the lifeline service include:

1. Installation of a primary access line including one modular jack, if required.
2. Provision of an allowance for an instrument.
3. Basic dial tone service.
4. Unlimited incoming calls.
5. Measured rate service, where it is offered, with an allowance of 30 calls per month. (Exception: Where measured service is not offered, flat rate service with unlimited local calls will be provided until such time as measured service is offered.)
6. Mileage charges (where applicable).[16]

Table 8.6
Telephone Rates and the Poor: The State Response

State	Prohibition Against Lifeline or Budget Rates	Lifeline or Budget Proposed	Implemented	Special Rates Available to	Cost
Alabama	No	No	No		
Alaska	No	No	No		
Arkansas	No	Yes	Yes	Food stamps only in areas LMS available	33% of 1-party RFR w/20 dir calls after 20 LMS rate
California	No	Yes	Yes	Income x 11,000	50% of basic flat rate
Colorado	Yes	No	No		
Connecticut	No	No	No		
Florida	No	No	No		
Georgia	Yes	Yes	Yes	Everyone	25 calls at a flat rate, after 12¢ call
Hawaii	No	No	No		
Idaho	No	Yes	Yes	Everyone	BLM $4.00 flat, $.04 initial minute + $.015 additional minutes
Illinois	No	Yes	Yes	Everyone	Optional & mandatory local measured service (ch=$4.50, sub. $6.00 flat component) + distance sensitive
Indiana	Yes	No	No		
Iowa	No	Yes	No		

Table 8.6
(Continued)

State	Prohibition Against Lifeline or Budget Rates	Lifeline or Budget Proposed	Implemented	Special Rates Available to	Cost
Louisiana	No	Yes	Yes	Everyone	LUMS 45% discount from basic exchange rate; standard M.S. 30% discount; message rate service 45%
Maine	No	Yes	Yes	Everyone	LUMS $4.81 w/30 mess. call/month, add. units are 11.4¢ each
Maryland	Yes	Yes	No		
Massachusetts	No	Yes	Yes	Everyone in 78% of exchanges	Optional LMS $3.25/month + 30 calls
Michigan	No	Yes	Yes	Michigan Bell subscribers	Two-party measured service $4.27/month w/44 call allowance, 10¢/call after 44
Minnesota	No	Yes	Yes		
Mississippi	No	Yes	Yes	Everyone in areas w/LMS	Low use LMS 55% of flat rate w/$3.00 month call
Missouri	No	Yes	Yes		
Nebraska	No	Yes	No		
Nevada	No	Yes	No		
New Hampshire	No	No	No		
New Jersey	No	Yes	Yes	Everyone in areas w/LMS	Optional low measured use service discount from flat rate w/20 mess. $3.65

Table 8.6
(Continued)

State	Prohibition Against Lifeline or Budget Rates	Lifeline or Budget Proposed	Implemented	Special Rates Available to	Cost
New York	No	Yes	Yes	Those who receive state aid and subscribe	50% of basic budget service
N. Carolina	No	No	No		
N. Dakota	No	No	No		
Oklahoma	No	Yes	No		
Oregon	Yes	Yes	Yes	Everyone	Budget measured service + time sen. usage charge; Stayton Corp. $5.78; PNWB $6.90; United Tel. $3.90
Pennsylvania	No	No	No		
Rhode Island	No	Yes	Yes	Only those served by NET	$5.88/month + charges based on time & length
S. Carolina	No	Yes	Yes		
S. Dakota	No	No	No		
Utah	No	Yes	No		
Vermont	No	Yes	No		

Table 8.6
(Continued)

State	Prohibition Against Lifeline or Budget Rates	Lifeline or Budget Proposed	Implemented	Special Rates Available to	Cost
Washington	Yes	Yes	Yes	Everyone	bPNWB two party budget local measured and BLM; United Tel; LMS
W. Virginia	Yes	Yes	No		
Wisconsin	No	Yes	Yes	Everyone	But service charges are waived for those meeting LIEA guidelines; $3.50 month + 24¢/call
Wyoming	Yes	No	No		

bPNWB has filed a lifeline proposal with the Utility and Transportation Commission eligibility based on public assistance or being 65 or older and low income; based on Basic Measured Service Rate and preselection of five numbers with unlimited calling privileges. Funded by other PNWB rates.

Note:
BBR	=	Basic Budget Rate
BLM	=	Budget Low Measured Service
LIEA	=	Low-Income Energy Assistance
LMS	=	Local Measured Service
LUMS	=	Low Use Measured Service
Mess.	=	Message Rate
M.S.	=	Measured Service
NET	=	New England Telephone
PNWB	=	Pacific North West Bell
RES.	=	Residential
RFR	=	Residential Flat Rate

Sources: National Association of Regulatory Utility Commissioners, Survey on State Lifeline Telephone Service, 1985, pp. 30-38, derived from Tables I, II and III. The Urban Center, College of Urban Affairs, Cleveland State University, "Telephone Lifeline Rates 1984," Energy Assistance Programs in the 50 States: 1984 Survey Update.

The costs of the program are covered through a state fund generated by a 4 percent surcharge on intrastate long distance calls. The fund was established with approximately $74 million. In 1984, 190,000 of the estimated 670,000 customers certified themselves and qualified for the program.

The Arkansas Response

The Arkansas Public Utility Commission instituted a targeted lifeline rate providing households that are food-stamp-eligible a rate that is approximately one-third that of basic flat rate residential service. The tariff is being provided to approximately 1,000 customers of the major telephone company in the state, which serves 65 percent of the total customers. The remaining residential customers make up the shortfall in revenues from the lifeline tariff. The regular residential subscribers are therefore subsidizing the customers utilizing the lifeline tariff.

THE JOINT FEDERAL-STATE RESPONSE

Along with the initial responses at the state level related to the "lifeline" issue was the convening of a federal-state Joint Board comprised of representatives of the FCC and state commissioners. In October 1985 the board adopted recommendations for cooperatively developing lifeline assistance programs. What emerged from these discussions of key stakeholders were strong incentives for the states to devise and implement lifeline programs. The states were not required to participate, but could initiate programs when appropriate. Under the plan, The FCC matches state assistance for low-income households under qualifying programs up to the amount of the federal subscriber line charges (the access charges). The program is voluntary and states have the option of participating. The announcement of the Joint Board action went on to state:

Although census data demonstrates that telephone subscribership levels have remained stable since the AT&T divestiture, and the pace of local rate increase requests has declined substantially in 1985, the Joint Board recognizes that, should substantial rate increases occur, it would be more difficult for low-income households to afford telephone service. As a result, the Joint Board recommended that the FCC adopt measures to supplement state assistance programs.[17]

By early 1987, 11 states plus the District of Columbia had submitted programs and had been certified by the FCC's common carrier bureau for this program.

Therefore with the schedule that has been agreed to for implementing the access charges, this lifeline assistance could result in a qualifying individual receiving "lifeline support" up to the following limits depending on the nature of the program implemented by the state.

	FCC	State	Total	One-Time Payment Limit
1986	$2.00	$2.00	$4.00	$30.00
1987	2.60	2.60	5.20	30.00
1988	3.20	3.20	6.40	30.00
1989	3.60	3.60	7.20	30.00

The federal contribution would be recovered through the carrier common-line charge.

The Joint Board took further actions in March 1987 that established an implementation schedule for subscriber-line charges through 1989 and expanded the lifeline programs to include assistance for low-income households in offsetting the initial charges associated with connection and installation of new service. The program referred to as "Link Up America" has two parts:

(1) qualified households are eligible for discounts of up to one-half of the charges assessed by local telephone companies for commencing service, up to a maximum of $30.00; and (2) payments to telephone companies to offset the interest cost of deferred payment plans for commencement charges.[18]

The new program is aimed at addressing the more than 5 million low-income households that currently do not have telephone service.

The Private Sector Response

At the winter 1985 meeting of the NARUC Subcommittee on Telecommunications, a representative of the FCC reported that the telephone companies were the "first line" of defense against the perceived threat to universal service. He urged that rather than further polarizing the congressional debate on lifeline telephone service, it was in the national self–interest for companies to come forward with policy and tariff proposals to avoid significant customer drop off. In his view, the second line of defense was the states.[19]

In forums ranging from PUC proceedings involving formal rate and tariff requests to generic legislative hearings, a variety of approaches has been put forth by telephone companies to deal with the increasing concerns of federal and state officials regarding telephone rate increases.

These proposals have been put forth in a turbulent telecommunications environment created by the aftermath of divestiture, rapid technological changes in the industry, and pressures of increased competition.[20]

While this turbulent environment and changes that have characterized the early 1980s in the telephone industry have led to a series of recent proposals, they were preceded by a decade in which the telephone industry and many state commissioners had begun shifting the historic basis upon which telephone service is used from a "value of service" philosophy to a "cost of service" philosophy. Simply put, value of service pricing is based on the relative value of the service to the customer rather than costs. Therefore, since telephone service was perceived to be more valuable for business customers than residential customers, the business customer paid more for the same service. The shift to a more realistic "cost of service" pricing philosophy and measured tariffs in contrast to flat rate tariffs had already created concerns with consumer groups and many state legislatures.

In the mid-1970s, legislation was considered to prohibit measured tariffs owing to the impact of rate increases attributable to the cost of service reforms for certain high-volume residential and business telephone customers. In one Ohio legislative hearing in 1977, several questions were raised by one of the authors of this book, David C. Sweet, for consideration of the lawmakers. These questions and factual observations contained in Appendix A to this book illustrate the dilemma confronting state regulators and legislators as political and economic pressures increased for more realistic, cost-based telephone rates.

Legislation seeking to prevent state PUCs from moving to cost-based pricing for telephone service was not enacted but this "evolutionary" reform has been caught up in the "revolutionary" reforms of divestiture and FCC-instituted access charges. While the impact of the evolutionary changes could have been accommodated and adjusted to over time, the sudden impact of local service increases associated with divestiture have catalyzed an increasing number of telephone users to demand a response.

The shifts in pricing philosophies had already developed concerns among certain telephone service stakeholders. With more recent events the number of stakeholder groups can join together in their self-interest, often for quite unrelated reasons, and bring political action to address their concerns.

Therefore, as the "first line" of response, it is critical that the telephone industry come forward in addressing a constructive set of options to deal with the plight of the low-income telephone users. The range of responses telephone companies are putting forth can be characterized both by the type of service or rate being offered and the eligibility criteria used in qualifying a customer for the service. The industry has played a key role in the negotiations that led to the recommendations of the Joint Board described in this chapter. Its role will be even more critical as the policy discussions shift to even further deregulation of telephone services. Appendix B contains a summary of the FCC-approved State Lifeline Assistance Programs that have emerged from the recommendations of the Joint Board.

Drawing upon definitions discussed earlier, a lifeline rate would be a subsidized rate (that is, below cost) and available to a targeted population (such

Figure 8.3
A Framework for Options: Lifeline Telephone Rates

Source: Compiled by the authors.

as the elderly or the poor).[21] Therefore, one way to characterize the range of possible responses that could be put forth by telephone companies is illustrated in Figure 8.3.

In constructing the framework identified in Figure 8.3, a range of possible options has been used. For example:

- *Arkansas*: Lifeline program rate is set at 33 percent of flat rate residential service. Lifeline program provides for 20 direct–dial calls but only in areas where standard local measured service is offered. Arkansas residents who receive food stamps through the state Department of Health Services are eligible for the program. [Note: All four states limit lifeline rate subsidies to the head of the household (that is, one phone).]

- *California*: Lifeline program rate is 50 percent of the area's flat rate service or 50 percent of measured rate service in areas where calls can be metered. Residents may participate in the program if their gross income is less than $11,000. [Note: Residents must certify themselves for the programs. In the cases of Arkansas, California, and New York, applicants must demonstrate their need.]

- *New York*: Lifeline rate is 50 percent of the basic budget rate. Residents who receive state financial aid are eligible to participate.

- *Wisconsin:* Lifeline service is priced at $3.50 per month plus 24 cents per call. There are no low-income restrictions for residents, although the service charge is waived for residents who are also eligible for the state's low-income energy assistance programs.

One of the most responsive set of options and lifeline rates has been offered by Pacific North West Bell (PNWB), which offers three types of low-cost telephone service to its Washington State residential customers: (1) budget local measured service, (2) two-party measured, and (3) basic local measured service. In 1984 PNWB filed a proposal with the Washington Utility and Transportation Commission that would also create a residential lifeline plan. Households would be eligible if they were recipients of assistance for the state, or if they were 65 or older and met the low-income guidelines, as defined by the states. The lifeline service would be based upon the Basic Measured Service rate, but would allow the subscriber to select up to five local numbers to which the subscriber would have unlimited calling privileges at no charge. What makes PNWB's proposal so interesting is that studies have shown that one-fifth of all outgoing calls go to the same receiving number. The next four numbers account for 30–40 percent of outgoing calls. Thus almost 50 percent of all outgoing calls go to only five numbers.[22]

With state–of–the–art telephone technology it may therefore be possible to provide a true lifeline service with unlimited calling and a significant subsidy, while at the same time restricting that subsidy to a predetermined set of telephone numbers and not, as has often been proposed, number of calls. Should this or related approaches become widespread, the inevitable debate will be: Who will pay the subsidy? As seen in the similar energy debates over the past decade the subsidy will become the responsibility of one of the various stakeholders in the process: the taxpayer (through government programs), the rate payer (through other utility services), the stockholder (through corporate contributions and reduced earnings), and the low-income telephone user (through restricted services).

Models exist and several programs have been implemented as a response to these major changes being confronted by the telephone industry and low-income telephone customers. With more than a decade of experience dealing with low-income energy issues it should be possible for utility regulators and policy makers to avoid the telephone assistance quagmire. Chapters 9 and 10 will summarize some of the lessons learned and possible applications in the decade ahead.

9

The Policy-Making Process:
Lessons Learned

THE QUAGMIRE

After hearing a presentation on energy assistance at a Cleveland community center in late 1979, an elderly woman explained that somehow the previous year she received assistance in paying her (utility) heating bills, and she hoped she could get help in paying her fuel bills this year but she didn't know how to get it or where to go to find out. Unknown to her, she was confronted with Ohio's energy assistance quagmire, depicted in Figure 9.1. Unfortunately, her plight was not unique and this proliferation of programs was duplicated across the country.

From 1974, when the Federal Office of Economic Opportunity authorized local community action agencies to spend up to 10 percent of their general operating funds for energy-related activities, the quagmire rapidly emerged over the next five years. By 1979 a myriad of programs had been put in place by all levels of government, by public utilities, and by social service agencies. No single federal, state, or local agency was responsible for dispensing information, allocating funds, processing applications, or delivering benefits. In some cases one agency received funding, another accepted applications, another made referrals, and still another delivered services.

The quagmire was a natural result of the process by which energy assistance policies were developed and programs were operated. At all government levels, but particularly at the federal level, it took a series of crises to bring about responses to the need for energy assistance. The first crisis was the oil embargo of 1973, the second the severe winters of 1976–77 and 1977–78 in the Northeast and Midwest, the third was oil price decontrol, and the fourth was deregulation of natural gas prices. Each crisis brought political pressure, ad hoc policy and program development, and last-minute funding appropriations. Even if the appropriations had been sufficient, they

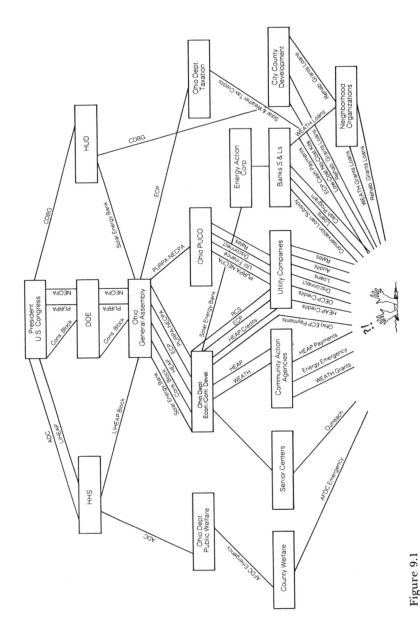

Figure 9.1
The Ohio Energy Assistance Quagmire

Source: Compiled by the authors.

were usually made too late to allow planning or coordinated distribution of benefits, a problem further compounded by late dissemination of federal regulations for states to follow in allocating their funds.

Since the authorization and appropriations supporting federal energy assistance policy were for only a one-year duration, most state and local officials were confronted with such programmatic and funding uncertainty that effective longer range planning was impossible. Energy assistance policy development is not unique in this respect. As Professor Thomas C. Schelling of Harvard University's Kennedy School of Government put it,

comprehensive wars on poverty notwithstanding, the rule [under the American approach to poverty] is to take a little care of the poor in each of multifarious policy domains rather than in a focused and unified way. The approach is piecemeal— fragmented, uncoordinated, and opportunistic. . . . As long as this unbudgeted and unconsolidated approach to public assistance is embodied in a vast entanglement of laws and agencies, lobbies and interests, and nobody can tell how adequate or inadequate it is in total, or which beneficiaries are getting more than their proper share or very much less, the system invites myopic efforts to deal with local deficiencies rather than comprehensive efforts to deal with global imbalances. Anyone who believes that the system is globally inadequate can typically do something about it only by providing more of the particular ingredient of assistance that his or her program disposes of.[1]

This aspect of American social policy development is ironically beneficial, in a sense, to energy assistance. Because the prices of energy have affected all Americans, and because the effects were felt sharply rather than gradually, energy assistance programs have developed a more broad-based constituency than other social welfare programs. In a political climate unfavorable to general welfare and assistance programs, seeking to keep energy assistance an energy issue rather than a poverty issue was successful in increasing resources and programs focused on this area. This pragmatic reality should not be lost sight of by those seeking to address the analogous "crisis" related to the significant increase in local telephone rates.

Given economic trends, the natural constituency for energy assistance also seems likely to grow. Energy prices, especially with natural gas price decontrol, will continue to rise although perhaps at a slower rate. If unemployment levels continue to reach relatively high levels more Americans will join the ranks of the poor and near-poor. With poor national economic growth, federal, state, and local governments' budgets will remain strained. The tendency will be to limit the increases in, or even cut back on public assistance, giving rise to a greater need for help with energy bills among a growing population.

In addition to the disfavor into which general assistance programs have fallen, the political mood seems to be one of shifting responsibilities away from the federal government to the state and local levels and to the private sector. President Reagan's New Federalism proposals embody that mood and create a new locus of responsibility for policy making in confronting issues such as energy or telephone assistance for the poor.

In spite of this shift in the policy-making setting, the federal government's energy assistance policies and programs already have created twin dependencies. The state and local governments have come to depend on federal funding to provide energy assistance; and poor consumers have come to depend on energy assistance. The transition from an emergency assistance program to help out in crises to a permanent entitlement program was reflected in the 1981–82 Low-Income Home Energy Assistance Program. A recent survey documented that over 90 percent of all energy funding being administered by the states comes from LIHEAP.[2] As has been the case with other social welfare programs, dependency will be hard to overcome.

Furthering the dependency syndrome, the federal government has focused on direct aid, helping the poor pay their fuel bills primarily through payments to their fuel suppliers. By creating an expectation that fuel bills will be paid, the federal government has in effect created a never-ending need for energy assistance. If fuel bills will be paid by the government, there is less incentive for consumers to conserve, and not as much reason for other public and private agencies to try other approaches to offset the burden on the poor. Similar trends have been found at the state government level where many have shifted their emphasis from direct assistance to weatherization and conservation.

In addition, the states have increasingly relied on direct payments to fuel vendors rather than aid directly to poor consumers—the vendor-line-of-credit approach. These trends are understandable. Sending a check to a utility company covering thousands of customers is easier than assessing needs and helping install appropriate conservation materials. More consumers can be served with a smaller expenditure for each. The result, however, is the creation of a continuing need by a dependent population, unless policy incentives are devised to effectively link grants or low-interest loans for installing conservation materials along with direct payment of utility bills.

In short, what began as a well-intentioned response to a series of real crises became an institutional bog, with a great many of those most in need not being served. The number of eligible people receiving LIHEAP benefits varies by state; it ranged from 15 percent in Nevada to 57 percent in Maine in Fiscal Year 1985.[3] An estimated 50 percent of those eligible are served in the Ohio Energy Credits Program, considered one of the best administered in the country. The number receiving conservation and weatherization assistance is even lower. An estimated 12 percent of those eligible for weatherization assistance were served as of Fiscal Year 1986.

The system is characterized by a series of overlaps and gaps. Different agencies offered duplicative services while few agencies offered any real help to such consumers as low-income renters. Most important, the system defeated its own purpose of reaching those most in need because of continuing lack of awareness and understanding by the poor about what kind of help is available and where to get it.

MAKING ENERGY ASSISTANCE POLICY

While energy assistance policy developed in a fashion similar to other social welfare policies, there are some important differences. A review of the factors that make energy assistance policy development unique offers some important lessons.

First, energy prices traditionally have been regulated by the government. Because of the importance of energy supplies to the country's development and our national defense, the federal government controlled domestic fuel prices and continues to regulate energy production and distribution. State regulatory agencies have long controlled energy prices set by public utilities. Because of this history of government control, it is arguable that government has a special responsibility to offset the impact of higher energy prices particularly those caused by decontrol.

Because much of the energy used for residential purposes is supplied by regulated monopolies, it is arguable that government, especially state regulatory agencies, has a responsibility to protect consumers from sharp increases, particularly those resulting from poor utility management practices. In this view, consumers should not bear the brunt of higher prices resulting from, for example, overconstruction or speeded-up construction of generating capacity owing to poor predictions of future electric needs, or from suspended construction of nuclear power plants, or for unrealistic purchasing practices of wholesale fuel supplies.

Yet assistance programs were an "afterthought" to the federal government's energy policy and were never incorporated into our nation's broader energy goals. This created delays in designing a federal response to the problem, which in turn resulted in the haphazard proliferation of programs—the quagmire—from which we are now only beginning to emerge.

The federal government is a critical, but not the exclusive, public–sector stakeholder in energy assistance. The development of policies and programs must be a shared responsibility with state and local government. However, the federal government is the only level with sufficient resources to equalize the impact of rising prices across the nation. It is the only level that can assure a minimum benefit across states. Because the impact of rising energy prices varies so much from state to state, state and local governments are in the best position to tailor programs to meet their individual needs, and the private sector should be the innovator, testing new approaches and providing funds.

Second, sharp disruptions in energy prices and supplies during the 1970s affected more consumers more drastically than changes in other commodities deemed essential to life. This gave rise to a large, diverse constituency and greater political pressure to provide aid to those burdened by energy costs.

This broad constituency was unified in its call for government support of energy programs but was adversarial in its demands for what form this assistance should take. The failure to define a common ground was a significant barrier to designing coordinated and effective programs. All agreed that it was a legitimate function of government to help people heat their homes, especially the elderly and the disabled—certainly more acceptable than increasing assistance for welfare mothers—but few agreed on how this help should be paid for and delivered.

Third, it is argued that the poor suffer more when energy prices increase than they do when the prices of other goods rise. Low-income individuals often have little or no control over the energy they consume making it more difficult for them to cut back on energy use to offset energy price increases. At the same time, their incomes are less likely to keep pace with energy price rises. Their housing stock is older, in worse condition, and more expensive to weatherize. Finally, their incomes are such that they do not have capital to invest in conservation materials or equipment. These factors increase the relative burden on low-income energy consumers to an extent not duplicated in other areas.[4]

Other structural factors increasing the burden on the poor include traditional pricing structures and credit and delivery systems. Although much has changed, the poor were penalized by pricing structures that charged less as energy use increased and payment systems that required that fuel be purchased before use rather than as used. In addition, the poor are less able to cut back fuel use or save by shifting to cheaper fuels because energy used for household heating generally is not discretionary or subject to easy substitution.

For these reasons, we have yet to develop an effective supply-side solution to the energy problem. Lifeline rates have failed for two reasons. First, utility companies have shied away from targeted rates based on income owing to problems with income verification and revenue recovery. Second, rates based on consumption (conservation rates) do not necessarily benefit the poor, who lack the resources to conserve. Thus rate reform efforts have had only minimal impact on the poor.

A strategy is needed that takes into account the special needs of the low-income groups. A solution that focuses on assistance payments must also be accompanied by a focus on efficiency of use (e.g., conservation). Only when low-income households gain control over the amount of energy they use will rate-related strategies be effective. The need for direct assistance, which is essentially a very expensive income transfer program, will continue unless we find a way to give people the resources—financial and technical—to control the amount of energy they use.

Fourth, the impact of energy prices varies widely across the country. While it is generally true that those in colder climates consume more and pay more, variations in the price of different fuels also have an impact. Consumers in the North Central region, for example, use more fuel than those in the Northeast, but Northeasterners pay more because they use more expensive fuel. Similarly, Floridians pay a high price for electricity for summer cooling and consume much more than those in other regions. Prices are expected to rise in the growing states in warmer climates, as electric generating plants are built to keep pace with increasing demand. In addition to location, there are wide variations in individual poor consumers' needs based on the type of housing in which they live, their family size and life-style, and the fuel available to them.

Although the poor and elderly are concentrated in central cities, making energy assistance an urban problem, rural residents are also at a particular disadvantage because of disruptions in energy prices and supplies. Rural consumers "are at the end of complex distribution webs and if anything happens to either price or quantity at any place within the web, the effect is amplified by the time it reaches rural consumers, farm firms, or small, isolated retailers and manufacturers," according to one analyst.[5] Other factors magnifying the impact of energy prices on rural areas include the large amounts of energy needed for many agricultural activities and the effect on small communities of the stimulated development of energy resources.

A similar example of the difficulty of targeting energy assistance to specialized regional and local differences is the federal government's late recognition of the fact that aid was needed for summer cooling as well as winter heating, a realization delayed until the heat wave of 1980 resulted in the deaths of some poor, elderly consumers. Therefore, the most effective and innovative policies have been tailored at the local or state level to address directly the vast differences that exist in energy assistance needs across the country.

Fifth, because energy assistance developed as an afterthought in our national energy policy, it has been plagued with having to fit between overlapping national goals. As market pricing of energy became the generally accepted means of meeting the national energy policy goals of efficiency and supply enhancement, the sometimes conflicting goal of equity got battered. The current political accommodation has been to emphasize efficiency in national energy policy because market-based pricing has encouraged both conservation and production of energy. The equity goal, meanwhile, is accommodated through income transfers. Most social welfare programs have a single, primary goal: to help the poor pay for the necessities of life. But energy assistance carries the weight of both helping the poor cope with higher costs and facilitating such national energy policy goals as conservation, efficiency, and supply enhancement. Direct assistance thus is criticized for its failure to provide incentives for conservation. Deregulation of natural gas, despite its impact on prices, is sought for efficiency and supply enhancement reasons.

Indicative of the skewed perspective on energy assistance have been proposals to include energy aid provided by the public and private sectors as income in determining the need for welfare payments. Such schemes effectively deprive the poor of help by offsetting the assistance received with reductions in welfare benefits. Receipt of energy aid might even make a poor consumer ineligible for welfare benefits.

Existing policy sends conflicting messages to recipients. Households are guaranteed a minimum level of assistance regardless of the amount of energy they conserve. Yet the shortage of money available for conservation makes any attempted linkages between these programs ineffective.

Sixth, energy assistance policy making is made more difficult by the fact that many proposed solutions benefit the nonpoor as well. This is obviously the case with general price controls, and less obviously the case with rate reduction and lifeline programs or market-pricing coupled with direct aid to the poor. General rate reduction programs, such as some so-called lifeline rates, provide a below-cost rate for all consumers who keep their consumption below a certain level, regardless of their income. Higher energy prices and the higher returns on investments resulting from market-pricing are said to benefit the very high incomes because of their ownership of corporate stock. Meanwhile, most vendor line-of-credit direct assistance programs benefit utilities, which reduce their uncollectible accounts, as much as they benefit the consumers those utilities serve. If the energy assistance policies seek to assist only those who are most threatened by loss of service, effective targeting must be undertaken to restrict eligibility to this group. Commensurate with targeting comes a need to develop effective outreach programs to assure that the targeted population can access the assistance programs.

Seventh, the lack of reliable data has required that energy assistance policy be made in somewhat of a vacuum. In addition to the general problem of determining which of the poor should be served, effective energy assistance policy requires data on energy consumption by low-income consumers as well as variations in need by location, type of housing stock, prices of available fuels, climate, and characteristics of individual consumers. Such data have been virtually impossible to come by. Data also are needed on the cost-effectiveness of weatherization and alternative energy sources. That such information is lacking was illustrated in a 1980 General Accounting Office report that said that neither the U.S. Department of Energy nor the states knew how many homes had been weatherized under the federal programs nor did they know how much weatherization had reduced energy costs and consumption in low-income homes.[6]

Similarly, lack of data has been one of the reasons for the narrow scope of energy assistance. Inadequate information on the impact of indirect energy costs has been coupled with considerations of administrative efficiency and the visibility of poor and elderly consumers without sufficient heat. As a result, no aid is available to help offset increases in the costs of gasoline, fuels used for essential residential purposes other than heating, or energy used to produce other essential goods and services. Since many of these uses are as nondiscretionary as residential heating and cooling, the poor and elderly have been penalized by this narrow focus.

Finally, energy assistance policy making has been particularly difficult because of the number of participants and the diversity of their goals. The federal government, for example, has a far greater role in energy pricing, production, and distribution decisions than it does in similar decisions governing the price and availability of food, clothing, medical care, and social services. The federal government entered the realm of state regulatory authority over utility rates with the passage of the Public Utility Regulatory Policy Act of 1978. PURPA essentially required states to consider the primary national energy policy objectives of conservation, efficiency, and equity in utility regulation. Although it did not displace such traditional goals of the state regulatory process as providing a fair and reasonable rate of return on investment, PURPA highlighted social equity issues in a way that was unsettling to state regulators who viewed their role as primarily that of economic regulation, leaving social justice and income redistribution to the legislature. As state regulators considered energy assistance programs such as lifeline rates, state legislators also began to enter the field of energy policy making.

According to one report, there was a quantum leap in enacted energy legislation at the state level, from 30 laws in 1973 to 379 laws in 1977.[7] Many of these laws established or expanded the authority of state energy offices, consumers' counsels, and governors' offices to deal with energy-related problems. Local governments, meanwhile, were becoming increasingly concerned about the energy prices of their own operations. Utilities, facing growing consumer protests, in some cases recognized their own self-interest in energy assistance activities, beginning conservation and weatherization programs and assisting in administration of direct assistance. Nonprofit and community agencies and organizations entered the field of energy assistance to try to help alleviate a highly visible problem.

In fact, the states have always served as "laboratories for our democracy" and energy assistance programs are but just another illustration. Longitudinal research by Cleveland State University's College of Urban Affairs Energy Program has documented a variety of state initiatives in responding to the energy assistance needs of low-income households. The most recent report, *Trends Report of Energy Assistance Programs in the Fifty States, 1979–1984,* concludes that "innovation appears to be greatest at the state and local levels where stakeholders closest to the problem have an incentive to develop creative solutions."[8]

In summary, the setting for energy assistance policy making is a difficult one. As one analyst put it:

All the political and economic trends . . . are moving in such a way that our capacity to remedy the inequities caused by higher prices is declining. We simply do not have the political wherewithal. The trends in Congress are against more transfer programs whether they be cash or in kind. This trend runs counter to . . . our overall energy policy paradigm—which is to allow prices to rise, and then repair the inequities by means of transfer mechanisms.[9]

In spite of this pessimistic assessment, however, the final question in this political climate becomes, How can one draw on the lessons learned in tracing the emergence of the energy assistance quagmire to address related issues involving public utilities and the poor, such as the threat to universal telephone service? Chapter 10 seeks to draw some more encouraging conclusions.

10

The Policy-Making Process: A New Era

At the national level, energy assistance policy seems set, at least for the near future. Energy will be priced near the market to bring about efficiency in the use of scarce resources. Efficiency thus will help achieve the goals of greater energy independence, because high prices will stimulate production and energy conservation. The same appears to be true for telephone policy. Divestiture is in place, the FCC decisions on access charges are being implemented, cost of service rates are the trend, and local service rates are going up.

If history repeats, equity will squeeze in the back door through income transfer programs, lifeline rates, or other initiatives seeking to alleviate the disproportionate impact of price increases on certain groups in the population. Utility assistance programs thus become primarily a poverty assistance issue, although advocates will be well-advised to focus on what many regard as a basic right to such utility services as home heat and telephone service for essential communication. This approach takes advantage of a larger constituency and more favorable political climate for support.

The major issues in formulating effective utility assistance policies and programs will remain the same but they will take place in a new era, requiring new approaches. An increasing share of the burden of designing, operating, and funding the utility assistance programs will fall to the states. The era of New Federalism is one in which state and local governments, not the federal government, in conjunction with public utilities and the private sector will have greater responsibility for utility assistance policy making.

NEW FEDERALISM

It is the quagmire, in the broadest sense, that brought about the New Federalism proposal. Substitute any major federal policy initiative in the last decade or so, and a similar illustration can be drawn. In his State of the

Union Address in January 1982, President Reagan outlined the concept of New Federalism. While he did not use the exact term "quagmire," he did call for a dramatic shift in major program responsibilities, including energy assistance, from the federal to the state level. Implementation of this New Federalism concept has completely changed the setting for addressing a variety of domestic policy issues, and specifically public utility assistance programs.

William Baroody, Jr., president of the American Enterprise Institute, in his foreword to the book, *Excellence in Education: The States Take Charge,* commented:

The domestic policy role of Washington, which not long ago was accelerating, is giving way to the states. The change is occurring for two reasons. First, federal budget pressure is diminishing the capacity of the federal government to be all things to all people.

Second, and more important, the states today are at once more competent, more skillful, and more sophisticated than at any time in our history. . . . This development is of the utmost importance in the 1980s because it is becoming clear that Washington cannot accomplish all that it set out to do in the sixties. Federal policy in too many areas has produced an Uncle Sam who is jack of all trades and master of none. Recognizing this, the Reagan administration and a number of state governors, Democrats as well as Republicans, attempted to fashion a "New Federalism," a sorting out of responsibilities between Washington and state capitols. The conventional wisdom, however, is that "New Federalism" is a failure—the states refused to cooperate.

But as Doyle and Hartle point out, if it did not get enacted formally, New Federalism—in education at least—is a reality today in all but name. Helter skelter, without benefit of centralized planning, Washington's role in education is decreasing and the role of the states is increasing in importance. . . .

The shift from the federal government to state government . . . means that the problems and opportunities before us will be confronted differently than they would have been had Washington's role increased in importance. Indeed, the diversity and variety of America's "system" of public schools gives new meaning to the notion of "let a thousand flowers bloom."[1]

While Baroody's comments are in the context of a book discussing the states taking charge in the area of education, his theme could be applied to a wide variety of domestic policies and programs.

To further illustrate this point, Nathan and Doolittle, in an article entitled "The Untold Story of Reagan's New Federalism," summarized the results of a three-year longitudinal research study that monitored the response of state and local governments to federal government spending cuts on domestic programs in general and social programs in specific. They concluded:

Conventional wisdom holds that the Reagan administration was very successful in cutting domestic spending and shifting priorities to defense, but failed to obtain any real results on its federalism initiatives. In a word, we believe that his view is mistaken. In fact, the Reagan administration's domestic spending cuts, while significant in some areas, tend to be overrated in importance. And Reagan's federalism reform objectives, which are nearly forgotten in the public consciousness, now appear likely to have a substantial and lasting impact.[2]

The Nathan and Doolittle study monitored the impact of federal budget cuts and changes in 14 states and 40 local governments within them and observed, "We are impressed, as we look across the 14 case studies for our study on fiscal year 1983, that the Reagan period has seen a resurgence in the role of state government."[3]

Longitudinal research in the area of energy assistance programs drew similar conclusions:

It would be presumptuous to suggest that when the College's Energy Program began in 1978, with an exclusive focus on analysis of state and local policy and program initiatives in the field of energy assistance, the program staff was predicting the proposed massive shift in responsibility from federal to state and local governments called for in the President's "New Federalism" proposals. It was, however, clear at that time that many innovative programs were being put in place by state legislatures and governors, as well as by local officials, agencies, and utilities, in many cases without federal funds. These innovative programs were overshadowed, and in fact overwhelmed, by federal programs and resources for energy assistance.[4]

Therefore as a result of New Federalism initiatives, accelerated by federal budget balancing measures such as the Gramm-Rudman Act, there is a new setting for dealing with utility assistance programs for the poor. No longer can we look to Washington and say "Solve it!"

THE NEW POLICY-MAKING SETTING

While historians will reflect on the Reagan era as one in which the concept of new federalism was implemented, as suggested by Baroody earlier, the concept has had bipartisan support. It also is not a new idea. For example, in 1971 the newly elected governor of Ohio, John J. Gilligan, a liberal Democrat, stated before the Joint Economic Committee of the U.S. Congress:

While federal action on many fronts is welcome, needed and indeed demanded by the States, there are limits to what the Federal Government can achieve. The Federal Government does not have the administrative apparatus in individual states and communities to do the job of state and local government. More important, Federal actions cannot be tailored to the many different situations of the several states and communities. . . . The new Administration of the State of Ohio asks for nothing more than the opportunity to meet its responsibilities, to bear its full share of the problems, to do the job that only state government can do, in cooperation with government at the local and federal levels. We don't want to come to you as mendicants, but as full partners in a new and vigorous Federal–State relationship.[5]

A new approach was being called for, one that assigns the responsibility for raising and spending revenue to the same level of government—a sorting out of both revenue–raising and program–implementation responsibilities.

Compare the thrust of Governor Gilligan's statements over a decade earlier, with the call for New Federalism as stated by President Reagan:

Our citizens feel they have lost control of even the most basic decisions made about the essential services of government, such as schools, welfare, roads and even garbage collection. They are right.

A maze of interlocking jurisdictions and levels of government confronts average citizens in trying to solve even the simplest of problems. They do not know where to turn for answers, who to hold accountable, who to praise, who to blame, who to vote for or against.[6]

The basic thrust of New Federalism, on which the crucial budget balancing debates must focus, is whether the Congress will be willing to yield both programs and revenue sources to state and local governments. One without the other will be a sham. If both do return, the challenge for the states will be to use the returned revenue sources and responsibilities to develop programs sufficient to meet the needs of their citizens.

Nathan and Doolittle have put the state response to the realities of New Federalism in three categories: (1) a pronounced response (for example, a major state initiative), (2) a state supplement to replace the federal program cuts, and (3) an opportunity to confront severe fiscal conditions by raising new revenues. Specifically, their study observed:

All 14 states in the sample for our study responded to the opportunities for a greater role, though in different measure and in different ways. Eight states made what we consider a pronounced response to the opportunities for increased influence created by the Reagan administration's federal aid policy changes. Three states (Massachusetts, New York, and, to some extent, New Jersey) supported many of the federal programs that were cut or would have been affected by the Reagan proposals and had the fiscal resources to fill the vacuum that the cuts created. Arizona and Florida—both conservative, fast-growing states—had governors who supported Reagan's decentralization objectives, and both states acted in several areas to take advantage of these changes. Three states (Missouri, Ohio, and Washington) faced severe fiscal conditions and viewed the New Federalism as an opportunity to confront them.[7]

Many state energy assistance programs were also designed to fill in funding and programmatic gaps in federal programs. They aided people not reached by federal programs—for example, the elderly and disabled; or they provided services such as low-cost weatherization that were not allowed under federal programs. As described in earlier chapters, however, many states also developed innovative programs in response to the energy assistance needs of the poor.

Although it is generally true that states hardest hit by energy price and supply disruptions have been most active and innovative in energy assistance, other factors enter the picture as well. As Mary Procter of the U.S. Office of Technology Assessment pointed out, "political concern at the state level seems to be determined by government traditions rather than necessarily by the degree of hardship."[8] Among the most active states have been Oregon and California, which have relatively mild climates, but where "there is a tradition of expecting state governments and local governments to be involved heavily in resource development and particularly in control of the electric generating industry." The same trend has emerged in dealing with the telephone assistance issue, again with California taking the lead.

In the era of New Federalism, all stakeholders must be involved; but in order to avoid the adversarial climate that resulted in the quagmire, it is crucial for the key stakeholders to take a leadership role in defining policy objectives.

Earlier in this chapter the suggestion was put forth that the quagmire, broadly defined, led to the New Federalism proposal. In the energy field, the decade of the 1970s was one of dramatic price increases because of ravaging inflation, decontrol, and international agreements among supplier nations. It was also a period of consumer awakening, consumer advocacy, and adversarial relationships between consumers, business, utilities, and government. In the energy utility field, it was a classic textbook case of confrontation: the consumer versus the utilities, corporate interests versus those of senior citizens, the manufacturers' associations versus the welfare rights organizations, and citizens for clean air versus the electric utilities. During the 1970s, consumers, senior citizens, and others involved in the advocacy movement made substantial gains—even though their energy costs continued to skyrocket. Just as the setting has changed, however, so has the approach that must be taken. Summarizing this period, Richard Vietor in his book, *Energy Policy in America Since 1945,* concluded:

What stands out is the inefficiency of the policy process; it could not have been more inept. The adjustment to high-cost energy, and the issues of equity that entailed, was certainly a difficult challenge. But the legislative and administrative problems . . . can only be attributed to institutional failure—the exclusive reliance on adversary process to make micro-economic policy.[9]

While it has always been the case that a utility company's stockholders and the consumer movement, as well as the other stakeholders, have many overlapping interests, during the 1970s they were not being defined and built upon—only their differences were being exploited in a setting of confrontation.

THE STAKEHOLDER APPROACH

The new policy setting will require a new approach. Leadership must come from a variety of stakeholders, with utilities taking major responsibility because they occupy a highly visible position. Many utility executives will respond: "We're a business, not a social service organization." However, in this new era, it may be an essential component for achieving more traditional "bottom line" corporate objectives to assume a leadership role in confronting low-income issues. R. Edward Freeman has suggested incorporating a stakeholder approach as part of a strategic management process aimed at achieving key corporate objectives.[10]

A stakeholder is any group or individual who can affect or is affected by the achievement of an organization's objectives. The notion that management need be responsive only to "stockholders" is broadened through this approach to include customers, suppliers, employees, unions, governments, local communities, and activist groups. From a strategic perspective, managers must deal with all of these groups who can affect the formulation and implementation of the firm's goals. A stakeholder map of one firm in the telecommunications industry is outlined in Figure 10.1. By specifying stakeholders and their stakes in detail, managers can formulate strategies for accomplishing stakeholder related goals, or at least better understand how stakeholders behave.

Using the stakeholder approach, Freeman recommends that an assessment be made of the "cooperative potential" and "competitive threat" of various stakeholder groups. He defines "cooperative potential" as:

the ability of a stakeholder group to help bring about the objectives of the firm, relative to other stakeholders, [and] "competitive threat" [as] the ability of a stakeholder group to prevent the achievement of a firm's objectives. The resulting matrix of relative cooperative potential and competitive threat yields four generic strategies for dealing with any stakeholder group [see in Figure 10.2]. A firm changes the rules by changing the basis for interaction with a stakeholder group. Depending on the circumstances and the countermoves that are available, such a strategy may include joint ventures, coalitions on issues of mutual interest, filing suit, getting legislation passed, or even using a third stakeholder as a coalition partner.[11]

At the heart of the stakeholder approach or strategy is negotiation. Freeman suggests:

Quite simply, if external groups can affect the firm, then bargains that are mutually beneficial must be sought. Secondly, dealings with the external environment must be interactive. The concept of strategic response plays a large role here. It is impossible to negotiate without anticipating the response of others, and in the absence of communications with stakeholders such anticipation will be at best a guess. Finally, the concept of strategy as outlined here implies that each party, both industry member

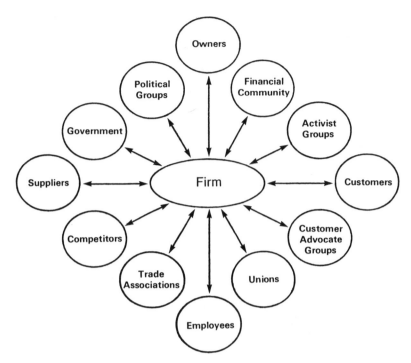

Figure 10.1
Stakeholder Map of a Telecommunications Firm

Source: R. Edward Freeman, "Managing the Strategic Challenge in Telecommunications,"
Columbia Journal of World Business 18 (Spring 1983):10. Reprinted with permission.

and other stakeholders, will seek to change the rules of the game whenever one stakeholder gains too much power. Through preemption, formal legislative initiative or other tactics, players will seek to regain control over their own affairs. Such natural responses make the concept of strategy in this conception critical to success in industries where the balance of power is up for grabs.[12]

As illustrated in Figure 10.1, a critical part of the stakeholder approach is two-way communication and the achievement of mutual benefit. While there is clear evidence that a stakeholder approach can work in confronting the responsibility of one utility to its stockholders, can a similar approach work in confronting issues of low-income customers? Who are the stakeholders that must be involved in addressing these utility assistance issues? They include:

Low Income Households	Utilities
Social Service Agencies	Management
Senior Citizens	Employees

Welfare Advocacy Groups	Employers
Neighborhood and Local	Unions
Development Groups	Board of Directors
Charitable Organizations	Stockholders
Local, State, and Federal	Long-Distance Carriers
Government	Utility Industry Suppliers and
Utility Regulatory Commissions	Equipment Managers
Construction Industry	Utility Customers
Foundations	Residential
Taxpayers	Commercial
	Industrial
	Financial Institutions

As was suggested in Chapter 8, if telephone customers are disen-franchised by rising costs associated with deregulation and divestiture, at-tempts will be made to deny the utility the power to deny a "basic right" to such customers. Ultimately the telephone utility will be called upon to pro-vide a remedy or suffer the impacts of the adversely affected stakeholders who band together in these troubled times in terms of telecommunications. As Freeman suggests, "It is in the interest of no one for customers to exit the market place . . . steps must be taken (by telephone utilities) to insure that disenfranchisement does not become the issue that ruins the path to deregulation."[13]

Therefore, with the federal court and FCC decision in place, if implemen-tation of deregulation and divestiture are the corporate objectives, a tele-phone utility must also confront the responsibility of addressing their social costs—not as a social service agency but as part of a successful corporate strategy. Some progress in this regard is being reported, such as a recent editorial in the Cleveland *Plain Dealer* entitled: "Is Divestiture Working?" which illustrated that a utility company taking the initiative to negotiate with stakeholders can reach an accord even in a highly charged political en-vironment:

Divestiture continues to be corporate rather than consumer friendly. If the low rates threaten AT&T competitors, they also threaten subscribers who hope to benefit from increased competition. For consumers (unable to afford even that shred of op-timism) the breakup is pushing costs up. Divestiture is supposed to have an opposite effect.

Locally, Ohio Bell and the Senior Citizen Coalition have agreed on phone rates for those over 65. The charge would be $11 for the first 90 calls per month and 15 cents for each additional call. Mayor Voinovich has asked the Public Utilities Commission of Ohio to order a basic rate of $3.70 a month plus 7 cents for the first 30 calls and 15 cents for each additional call. *Basic math shows that for 90 calls, the Ohio Bell agree-ment is cheaper.*

Let the elderly decide whether the greater flexibility of the city plan outweighs its higher cost. And we will leave it to PUCO and Ohio Bell (for the moment, at any rate)

HIGH

Change the Rules Programs	**Offensive Programs**
1. Formal rules changes through government. 2. Change the decision forum. 3. Change the kinds of decisions that are made. 4. Change the transaction process.	1. Change the beliefs about the firm. 2. Do something (anything) different. 3. Try to change the stakeholder's objectives. 4. Adopt the stakeholder's position. 5. Link the program to others that the stakeholder views more favorably. 6. Change the transaction process.
Defensive Programs	**Status Quo Programs**
1. Reinforce current beliefs about the firm ("preach to the choir"). 2. Maintain existing programs. 3. Link issues to others that stakeholder sees more favorably. 4. Let stakeholder drive the transaction process.	1. Do nothing and monitor existing programs. 2. Reinforce current beliefs about the firm. 3. Guard against changes in the transaction process.

RELATIVE
COOPERATIVE
POTENTIAL

LOW

HIGH   RELATIVE COMPETITIVE THREAT   LOW

Figure 10.2
Generic Strategies for Stakeholders

Source: R. Edward Freeman, "Managing the Strategic Challenge in Telecommunications," *Columbia Journal of World Business* 18 (Spring 1983):12. Reprinted with permission.

to devise a similar formula for the poor. Ohio Bell seems to have recognized the need to help shield the elderly from the inevitability of rising rates. The poor are no less vulnerable, and no less deserving.[14]

The proposal referred to for senior citizens was not implemented when other interested stakeholders could not agree to the proposal. However, the leadership responsibility of the utilities is clear in a stakeholder approach, and it must be a continuing commitment to find a common ground for addressing the needs of the low-income customer. At the same time, there are other groups of equal importance. For example, at the state level, addressing social equity issues such as utility assistance programs traditionally has been thought to be the domain of the legislative arm. Increased consumer pressure and federal and state legislation required state utility regulatory bodies, which traditionally focused exclusively on economic regulation of the utilities, also to devote more attention to social equity problems. The concept underlying lifeline rates, for instance, was expressed in California's Miller-Warren Energy Lifeline Act of 1975 as "Light and heat are basic human rights and must be made available to all people at low cost for basic minimum quantities."[15]

A 1979 report by an Ohio legislative committee is also representative of the changed perspective of state regulatory responsibilities, saying:

In the past, the justification for utility rate structures has over-emphasized economic requirements such as the utility's revenue needs or the allocation of economic resources. As the cost of energy has increased, the consideration of the social justice issues associated with the equitable allocation of costs among consumers has become especially important.[16]

Several approaches have been taken to reconcile the differing goals of the many stakeholders involved or potentially involved in utility assistance policy making at the state level.

In Michigan, a package of legislation was enacted that met the self-interests of many of the groups involved in energy policy in a coordinated way. The legislation was developed in cooperation with the public utility commission, utility companies, and consumer representatives. It provided mechanisms for assuring utilities adequate operating expenses, assuring that customers paid a reasonable share of costs, assuring that new power plants were necessary before authorized, and assuring that low-income households got assistance. Each piece of legislation was tied to the others: either all were approved or all were defeated.

In Ohio, a series of symposia involving state legislators, regulators, program administrators, public interest groups, and utility company and consumer representatives developed options for better coordinating and operating existing energy assistance programs. The process purposely concentrated more on organizational structure than on utility assistance policy goals. Symposia participants felt that a structural focus would allow the state to meet the needs of low-income and elderly residents over time, to be flexible enough to accommodate changing federal and state policies and financial situations, and to provide continuity of benefits and services.

These initiatives that follow a stakeholder approach have some common components. First, they recognize the states as key stakeholders in policy making, particularly in the area of pricing and assistance programs. Second, the balance long-term objectives of reducing dependence and state reliance on federal funding with short-term emergency help, while focusing on coordination of all utility assistance efforts. Third, they take into account the interests of all stakeholders in developing the most acceptable and most effective programs. Fourth, they include the utilities as full partners in the process and many cases look to them to provide the critical leadership.

POLICY AND PROGRAM DIRECTIONS

In the past decade, national policy proposals for dealing with the problem of rising energy costs and the poor can be divided into at least these categories:

1. General price controls
2. Adding an energy component to general welfare assistance
3. The vendor–line of credit programs providing direct assistance to the poor population linked specifically to their fuel bills, on the theory that funds earmarked solely to provide needed fuel supplies are more politically acceptable than increased general assistance
4. Providing crisis assistance to prevent shut-offs
5. Providing grants, low-cost loans, and technical assistance for conservation measures
6. Mandating utility regulatory reforms

In confronting telephone and related utility assistance issues, the current political mood appears to rule out the first category of general price controls. As for increasing general welfare assistance, it appears more politically feasible to advocate specifically earmarked aid for utility costs (e.g., energy, telephone) than to advocate more money for the poor. It is unlikely that the federal government will be the source of major funding for utility assistance programs.

The third category of direct assistance is the current focus of many utility assistance programs, but it is widely criticized as failing to encourage conservation or more efficient use of the utility service—such as, energy, telephone service, and water—and tending to encourage a permanently dependent population. Conservation assistance appears to be the most fruitful long-

term solution, although such programs are undoubtedly the most compli-
cated and expensive to administer and have the least focused constituency.
Mandating utility regulatory reforms appears to have gained a solid accep-
tance as components of utility assistance policy at the state and federal levels
but are not very effective in targeting assistance to those in need.

While these debates will continue, we can take steps to learn from past
lessons in developing new policies in a new setting and with new approaches. Several of these possibilities are outlined below.

The One-Stop Approach

The quagmire was the inevitable result of a large number of public and
private policy makers seeking to put into place quickly programs to confront
the impact of the dramatic increase in energy costs on low-income households.

The states must now provide further leadership in developing well-
planned, responsive, manageable, and comprehensive programs to meet
the utility needs of their low-income households equitably. Using a stakeholder approach, public utilities have a shared responsibility to provide
much needed leadership in this regard at the local level along with local
governments, neighborhood organizations, and social service agencies.

The options available to the states include providing a minimum coordinating mechanism that would make recommendations for improved
coordination and program administration; coordinating long-range planning, policy development, funding, and coordination as Michigan did; and
administering all programs out of a single agency. At the local level, this
could translate into one-stop outreach, application, and information centers
where poor and elderly residents could find out about and determine
whether they are eligible for the full range of energy aid. This concept for addressing problems associated with the quagmire is illustrated in Figure
10.3.

In addition to centralized information and outreach centers, local
governments should take on primary responsibility for targeting programs
to reach those most in need and for linking existing benefits. Providing
direct assistance without conservation, for example, is an ineffective long-
term solution. Local governments can best make sure that those receiving
direct assistance are given priority for weatherization help. At the same time,
weatherizing an unrehabilitated home is less than effective. Again, local
government, in cooperation with local utilities, can best link weatherization
and housing rehabilitation programs.

Since in many cases public–sector programs do not provide sufficient
funding for outreach efforts, this may be an effective role for funding provided by utilities, foundations, and other social service agencies. Utilities,
libraries, and social service agencies should be equally versed in providing

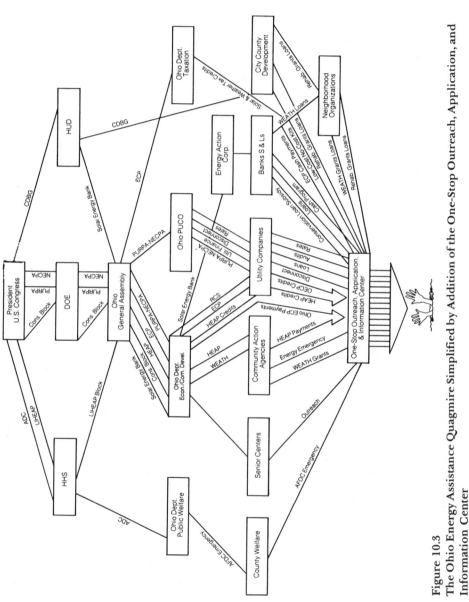

Figure 10.3
The Ohio Energy Assistance Quagmire Simplified by Addition of the One-Stop Outreach, Application, and Information Center

information and assistance for enrollment in all utility assistance programs. While it may be unique for a telephone company customer representative to help a low-income customer enroll in an energy assistance program, the potential mutual benefits are self-evident. Once developed, comprehensive directories and application procedures can be administered in a variety of one-stop centers at minimum cost. University outreach programs can be utilized in compiling the directories and providing training sessions for certain personnel.

Vendor Line–of–Credit Programs

Experience demonstrates that significant stakeholder constituencies can be rallied for instituting targeted direct assistance programs. Some type of direct assistance or lifeline service will inevitably be part of a comprehensive utility assistance program.

Who will pay for these programs? The most effective policies will entail the joining together of a number of stakeholders: low-income customers, utility companies, state legislatures, public utility commissions, and Congress. This stakeholder approach, illustrated below, recognizes that all parties have both rights and responsibilities.

- The customer has both the right to service and the responsibility of "conservation" in the use of that service.
- The utility has the responsibility of providing the service and the right to regain the revenue lost through any subsidized tariffs.
- The government, and specifically state legislatures, is the most effective focus for establishing social policy related to public utilities, and many have demonstrated their ability to establish criteria and appropriate revenues for these services (with the encouragement of stakeholder constituencies). State PUCs can also demonstrate leadership in initiating proposals and establishing a framework for company-initiated programs.

The source of the revenues to underwrite the lifeline subsidy inevitably will be the taxpayer or the ratepayer. The most straightforward way is a legislative or congressional appropriation from general tax revenues. An alternative tax to preserve universal telephone service as described by Reinking would be a head tax. He suggests that "local access line price increases" are similar to a head tax.[17] He argues that many current proposals for maintaining universal service call for an excise tax on telephone usage, specifically long-distance service. This is one of the most inefficient tax methods and "merely creates another way of recovering revenue from the telephone service."[18] In essence, it shifts the pricing of telephone service from the regulators to the legislators. As illustrated in Figure 10.4, the model vendor

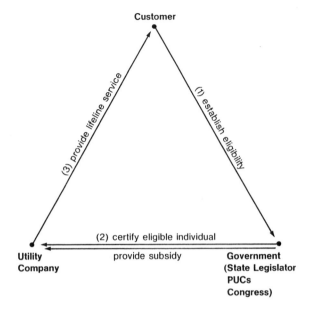

Figure 10.4
Vendor Line-of-Credit Model

line-of-credit program is based on the utility providing the lifeline service to a targeted population that is certified by an appropriate government agency and then being recovered from the revenue pool established to underwrite the subsidy.

Improved Targeting of Eligible Households

One barrier to effective targeting of utility assistance programs has been the restriction in most jurisdictions against "discrimination within a customer class." Court decisions rescinded some lifeline tariffs because of that restriction. Reinking has proposed one approach. His analysis concludes that "universal telephone service is provided to customers above the poverty line, but when viewed as a customer class, customers in poverty do not enjoy universal telephone service."[19] Using marginal cost analysis, he concluded that "from an economic perspective, the establishment of low-income lifeline service as a reasonable classification for pricing is within the scope and duties of regulatory bodies."[20]

Whether established by the regulator or the legislator, effective targeting must also be a part of a comprehensive approach to utility assistance programs.

Incentives for Conservation

Conservation is most often associated with energy assistance programs: using the energy resource more efficiently. However, there is another dimension of the conservation issue that affects all utilities—electric, gas, telephone, and water—and that is the conservation of capital. Utilities are confronted with enormous capital requirements in meeting demands for their services. For example, the estimated bill for telecommunication equipment will approach $100 billion per year by the end of this decade.[21] During the past decade electric and gas utilities were confronted with staggering capital requirements to build new facilities. Therefore, more efficient use of the utility service can result in reduced demands for new capital outlays.

This approach inevitably leads to requirements for improved forecasting of utility service requirements and the resultant construction schedules to meet these demands. In the past this has been the sole responsibility of the utility. However, in a shared responsibility approach, all stakeholders should have an opportunity to review and critique these planning forecasts.[22]

While capital conservation debates have most recently been focused on electric utilities, they are equally applicable to other utilities and specifically telephone companies.[23]

Historically, there has been little incentive for utilities to promote conservation. On the one hand this view was encouraged by the fact that in decades past, the marginal cost for a new utility plant was below the average cost. Therefore, new plant additions often lowered rates for consumers. It was an all-stakeholders-win situation: new plant, lower costs, lower rates, and oftentimes higher profits for the companies. Though that idyllic circumstance has long passed, in most states the overall policy guiding utility rate case decisions has not. The guiding principles of rate base regulation have sought to assure that the utility covers its operating expenses plus earns a reasonable rate of return on its "rate base."[24] Specifically, the formula states:

$$RR = OE + r(OC - D)$$

in which: RR = revenue requirements, OE = operating expenses, r = rate of return, (OC − D) = rate base valued at its original cost less depreciation.

The subject of this proposed reform will focus on one of the many issues that could be discussed. That is, a utility generates revenue by selling its services, not providing incentives or encouragement to customers to buy less of that service (for example, use it more efficiently). In the era of marginal costs being less than average costs, the formula worked—all stakeholders gained. More rate base meant lower rates and increased profits. What is needed in this new era is an incentive in the regulatory equation for profits to be gained by conservation measures. Oregon and Michigan, to name two states, have developed policies whereby conservation measures financed by utilities can be capitalized as part of the rate base—a much more effective incentive to conserve both energy and capital. As a result it would positively affect all utility customers, not just the poor. Similar efforts will have to be developed to provide incentives for more efficient use of telephone service in order to reduce the impacts of the anticipated need for massive capital investment on the part of the low-income customer.

DEREGULATION AND A NEW SOCIAL CONTRACT

Still another "reform" approach being proposed, especially in regard to telephone service, is complete deregulation with special consideration for addressing the needs of the poor. This concept has been labeled by some advocates as a new social contract. The concept of a social contract in regard to utility services encompasses the granting of an exclusive franchise to a company to serve all customers within a given area in exchange for economic regulation of their rates and services.

In 1985, V. Louise McCarren, chairman of the Vermont Public Service Board, stated: "It is time, then, to rethink the basic social contract and perhaps to remove regulators from the role of overseers of the transition from regulated monopoly to competitive environment.[25] Her proposal calls for local telephone companies to be deregulated, with no rate of return or price regulation, other than posting of rates and no franchise protection, in exchange for an agreed maximum percentage-per-year increase in residential- and small-business basic exchange rates. The basic objectives of the proposal would be to streamline the state's regulatory powers, maximize advantages presented by the new competitive environment in telecommunications, and prevent monopoly revenues from subsidizing competitive services.

Kahn supports this direction and believes that in the decade ahead "ways will be found to reconcile increasing deregulation and competition in the public utilities—telephone, electric and gas—with protection of captive (mainly residential and small business) customers."[26] In writing in support of the deregulation trend, Kahn states:

"Ultimately, I suspect that what we have to hope for is full deregulation of the competitive operations; sooner or later we have to get regulators out of the business of handicapping the process. That means we have to find ways of protecting captive customers, to the extent we think they continue to require protection, in ways that divorce their rates totally from the revenues that the regulated companies get in their competitive operations, and without perpetually restricting the kinds of activities those companies are permitted to undertake."[27]

In wrestling with the trend toward deregulation, Trebing suggests that:

"The most significant problem in the next decade will be the need to develop appropriate policies for coming to grips with changing market structures in electricity, gas, and telecommunications. Competition will be intense in some markets, while residual monopoly will remain strong in others. This will create a clear problem in protecting monopoly customers from price discrimination and cross subsidization, while giving the firm a degree of latitude to respond to competitive entrants. All of these pressures are clearly evident in electricity, gas and telecommunications. At the same time, there will be a need for long-term regulation to assure that this market structure, which is partially competitive and partially monopolistic, minimizes the cost to society. Public utility services will continue to be necessities and adequate service at minimum social cost will become a major public policy objective.[28]

However, Jones provides a note of caution that the trend toward deregulation in the guise of a new social contract should be clearly understood. In the monograph entitled "A Perspective on Social Contract and Telecommunications Regulation," Jones states: "Stripped of the favorable (or unfavorable) connotation of the label, social contract proposals in telecommunications are merely part of an array of initiatives for partial deregulation in the move to dismantle government oversight of economic processes."[29] At this point, substantial progress will have to be made in addressing numerous concerns of stakeholder groups.

Just as no one stakeholder group is capable of providing the required leadership in developing new policies and programs addressing the issue of public utilities and the poor, it is equally true that no one approach or model will be universally effective. Rather it is the process that is important. The development of energy assistance policies and programs over more than a decade demonstrates very clearly that when programs are developed with the involvement of all stakeholders, the chances for successful implementation improve. One major lesson learned is that when confronted with a crisis, innovative approaches adopted at the state and local level—with leadership provided by government officials, neighborhood leaders, utility executives, and community organizations working together—have provided models for national policy.

The FCC recognized the importance of this process in establishing its Joint Board. Although the Joint Board's policies have yet to be fully tested, many hope that they will serve as a base around which complementary programs can be built and will avoid some of the pitfalls met by the energy assistance programs. Similarly, energy assistance stakeholders have much to learn from the formulation of the concepts of universal service and social contracts in the telephone industry. While the reality will persist that the growing need for providing essential utility services cannot be met with dwindling resources, it is equally clear that the responsibility is shared by all stakeholders for devising effective public utility policies for the poor.

Appendix A: Testimony

Questions Regarding Prohibiting Measured Telephone Tariffs
before the Ohio Senate Energy and Public Utilities Committee
and the Ohio House Committee on Insurance, Utilities, and
Financial Institutions, Columbus, Ohio (1977)

Question:

Should the Ohio General Assembly block cost-based pricing for utility service in Ohio?

The Facts:

- Much of the current crisis in rapidly rising utility prices can be attributed to the way utilities have structured their rates over the past two decades. All the utilities—electric, natural gas, and telephone—have only recently been under pressure to relate more directly the cost of providing service to the price charged for that service. For example:

  - It costs twice as much to produce a kw of electricity at 5:00 p.m. as it does at 1:00 a.m.

  - One additional telephone call during peak hours costs $100–300 in additional investments in equipment and facilities.

  - The utilities' very successful campaign to encourage more and more consumption without cost-of-service pricing for several decades has now returned to haunt them. On the one hand, they're facing higher and higher capital financing costs to expand facilities to meet demand, while their customers demand to know why they can't continue to pay low rates for more service.

- Cost-of-service pricing—for all utility service—can return some control over rising utility bills to individual consumers. It is a fair way to charge for service: the more you use, the more you pay.

- Without cost-of-service pricing, consumers will continue to have little control over their utility bills, and efforts to conserve will probably result in even higher bills.

Question:

Should a rate structure be banned in Ohio that would ensure that basic telephone service is affordable for all Ohioans who need and want it five or ten years from today?

The Facts:

- In the last ten years, the average number of phone calls per customer and the average duration of time of those calls has grown 1.5 percent per year compounded annually. This increased usage increases the cost of supplying local service.

- To collect revenues to cover increasing costs, the utilities raised rates. Under a flat rate system, that increased cost is spread evenly over all customers within classes. Those rates have doubled since 1959:

Date	1-Party Flat Rate Res. (Columbus)
1-1-59	$ 5.50
4-1-70	6.80
8-14-73	8.00
8-13-76	10.70

- As flat rates continue to go up, what assurance will Ohioans on low or fixed incomes have that they won't be "priced out of the market"? Projected flat rates for residential telephone service in the Columbus area in the year 2000 range from $30 to $67 a month.

- Measured service rates can be constructed to offer a basic lifeline rate affordable by all Ohioans.

- In the 1977 Harris Survey of Bell system customers nationwide, a sizable majority (60–90 percent) said they would prefer a measured service (M.S.) rate over a flat rate that "would rise much faster and higher."

- To protect low– and fixed–income Ohioans, the PUCO ordered Ohio Bell to raise the call limit for its optional residential measured service from 15 to 30 calls (I proposed a 45–call limit).

Question:

Should a rate structure be banned in Ohio that would slow down the "revolving door" at the PUCO of larger and more frequent rate increase requests?

The Facts:

- Because telephone rate structures have for the most part had no relation to the actual cost of service, the increase in phone usage does not result in an increase in company revenues. So, as usage goes up faster, the utility applies for larger and more frequent rate increases.

- M.S. rate means the more a customer uses his phone, the more he pays— the cost of providing the service is the cost the customer pays for it. The company collects more revenues from heavy users, less revenues from low users, cutting down the need for frequent rate cases.

- Measuring number of calls is particularly important for cost-of-service pricing because the largest percentage of costs are included in getting a call under way.

- Because cost-of-service pricing is the most equitable, it should be applied to all utility rates in Ohio—gas, electric, water, and telephone.

- Legislation of specific rate structures will not necessarily protect Ohio consumers from excessive utility profits. What is required is legislative action to make sure the PUCO is continually monitoring profit levels and taking action when those levels become excessive.

Question:

Should a rate structure be banned in Ohio that would benefit Ohioans over 65 and Ohioans making less than $15,000 a year the most, and benefit Ohioans making over $25,000 a year the least?

The Facts:

- Those more able to pay rising telephone rates also make the most calls. Average number of calls made daily from home (Bell System):

All Households (average)	4.7
Under $7,009 a year	3.5
$7,000–$14,999	4.7
$15,000–$24,999	5.3

$25,000+	5.7
Professionals	5.6
Executives	5.3

Therefore, an M.S. rate based on number of calls would benefit the lower income, low user the most.

Question:

Should the option of measured service be taken away (as called for in S.B. 405) from the 200,000 Ohioans, including those under 65 or those on low and moderate incomes, who have already elected this rate?

The Facts:

- 200,000 residential customers have elected an optional M.S. rate (30–call limit) offered by Ohio Bell since 1976.
- More than 26 percent (largest percentage) of those 200,000 are over 64 years old. A total of 46 percent are 55 or over.
- About 50 percent of those 200,000 make between $7,500 and $15,000 a year. Another 35 percent make under $7,500 annually. In contrast, only 1 percent make between $25,000 and $30,000 and no families with incomes over $30,000 have elected M.S.

Appendix B: Summary of FCC-Approved State Lifeline Assistance Programs

SUMMARY OF REQUIREMENTS

—means test to determine eligibility: highly targeted assistance program which focuses on those individuals with limited incomes.

—subject to verification: procedures must be established which routinely check to ensure that those individuals eligible under the program are the individuals benefiting under the program.

—available for a single telephone line for the principal residence of eligible households.

APPROVED STATE PROGRAMS

—Arizona: establishes a three-year Telephone Assistance Pilot Program that targets individuals at or below 150% of federal poverty guidelines. State assistance includes: monthly base rate—unlimited calling, telephone rental $2.25; monthly wire and line maintenance fee; and one-time upgrade of service (not to exceed $27.50). All applicants are state interviewed and certified annually.

—Arkansas: establishes a Lifeline Measured Rate Service available to residential ratepayers who qualify under the federal food stamp program. The local program has been in effect since September 1984 and provides an estimated average benefit of $4.10 per month per subscriber, independent of the waiver of the subscriber line charge.

—Colorado: enacted legislation effective September 1, 1986, to establish the Colorado low-income Telephone Assistance Program through revised state statutes. The law provides single line dial-tone and flat-rate charge in a principle residence equivalent to a 25% discount. Eligible subscriber and state social service recipients of financial assistance programs for the elderly and low-income disabled persons who qualify for supplemental security under federal programs.

—District of Columbia: establishes an Economy II service available to residential ratepayers who are over 65 years of age and qualify under federal statutory criteria for participation in the Low Income Home Energy Assistance Programs or the Complementary Energy Assistance Program in the District. The local program provides an average benefit of $4.81 per month per subscriber, independent of the waiver of the subscriber line charge.

—Hawaii: enacted legislation on April 30, 1986. The rate is $2.70 less than the regular individual residence rates for eligible participants 60 years of age or older with total annual household income of $10,000 or less. On October 15, 1986, the Hawaiian Telephone Company filed tariffs to the Public Utilities Commission to set verification and income eligibility standards, provide installation of a single residence access line and associated equipment, a 50% reduction in service connection charges, elimination of nonrecurring charges, and three-month payment leniency or reduced connection charges.

—Idaho: The 1987 Idaho Legislature passed an act to provide an Idaho Telephone Assistance Plan (ITAP) to be effective July 1, 1987. Under ITAP, Idaho local exchange customers who qualify for Low Income Home Energy Assistance (LIHEAP) under regulations administered by the Idaho Department of Health and Welfare will receive a reduction in their monthly bills for basic exchange service of either $2.00 or the same amount as the Federal Communication Commission's subscriber line charge, whichever is greater. In no case may the discount exceed the rate charged for the grade of residential basic local exchange service subscribed to by each eligible individual. The Idaho Telephone Assistance Plan shall only be used to provide for a single residence line at the principle residence of the eligible subscriber. To participate in ITAP, applicants shall meet the following criteria: 1) head of household, 2) 60 years of age or older, and 3) participate in LIHEAP.

—Nevada: The Nevada Experimental Lifeline Program establishes two sets of criteria for eligibility. Each meets the federal criteria. The first requires the applicant to be at least 60 years of age and the applicant's household income limited to 150% of federal poverty levels for each household. The second requires the applicant to be a recipient of government-funded public assistance, e.g., SSI and SSA, regardless of age, limited to 150% of poverty level. The Experimental Lifeline Program will be funded solely by the shareholders of Nevada Bell to provide the $2.00 per month discount and the once-a-year 50% discount connection charge. Eligible subscribers will receive discounts without limitation to the grade of residence or customer calling patterns.

—New Mexico: Mountain Bell's Low Income Telephone Assistance Program (LITAP) in New Mexico was approved by the New Mexico State Corporation Commission, effective March 1, 1987. Under LITAP, Mountain Bell's customers who qualify for Medicaid benefits under regulations administered by the New Mexico Human Services Department will receive a $2.00 per month reduction in monthly bills for basic exchange service. The service and equipment charge to enter this program will be waived. Eligible customers are entitled to a 25% discount on the access line service and equipment charge.

—North Carolina: establishes a matching program in the state and is available to ratepayers who qualify under the federal AFDC and SSI programs. The program provides for a credit on the local service bill of 50% of the subscriber line charge, independent of the federal waiver.

—Ohio: The Public Utilities Commission of Ohio (PUCO) has recently approved the low-income "telephone assistance plans" (TAPs) of 8 local exchange companies. Each TAP plan offers a waiver of the security deposit and a 50% reduction in service connection charges upon initiation or reestablishment of service to participants in the Home Energy Assistance Program or the Ohio Energy Credits Program. The requirements in both programs have income limits per person and per household/per annum. In addition, eligibility for Ohio Energy Credits requires head of household and/or spouse to be age 65 or older, or permanently or totally disabled, with gross annual household income limited at $9,000. The TAP offerings are provided to eligible customers through the deposit waiver and connection discount only once in a one-year period. The Ohio tariff given each subscriber is applied monthly up to the SLC limit of $2.00. Where assistance under an LEC's TAP is less than SLC, the amount of nonrecurring state assistance will be set commensurate with a specified number of months.

—Oregon: establishes an Oregon Telephone Assistance Program (OTAP) available to ratepayers 60 years of age or older and qualified for the federal food stamp program. The program provides for a credit on the local service bill of $2.00, independent of the federal waiver of the subscriber line charge.

—Utah: established a lifeline program which addresses the price of local service and the customer's cost of obtaining telephone service. Telephone companies with rates for local service (not including extended area service, mileage charges for areas outside of the base rate areas, and optional features) above the funded portion of the standard needs budget for telephone time include Mountain Bell, Continental Telephone Company of the West, and Beehive Telephone Company. Other telephone companies may apply to the Public Service Commission of Utah for a lifeline rate if they desire to offer one.

Customers who qualify by income or are participating in any one of eight income-eligible welfare programs supervised by Utah's Department of Social Services may register themselves for lifeline services by filing a certificate with their local exchange carrier, if the carrier offers lifeline telephone service.

The telephone companies will, not less than annually, verify their lists of lifeline rate participants with the eligibility lists kept and maintained by Social Services of Utah.

—Vermont: enacted broad legislation on May 13, 1986, requiring the Public Service Board to adopt rates designed to implement a lifeline program and provide a $2.00 credit toward payment on monthly local telephone charges by eligible households. The legislation also required the Department of Social Welfare to continue to administer the eligibility and verification provisions of the program. Two paths of targeted eligibility are administered: first, participation in either AFDC, Food Stamps, Fuel Assistance, Medicaid, or Supplemental Security Income programs; second, through the Vermont Department of Taxes' state sales tax credit program for individuals over 65 years of age and having a gross income of less than $13,000 per annum.

—Washington: The lifeline bill was approved by the Washington State Legislature during the 1987 regular legislative session. It became effective July 26, 1987. Under the Washington bill, eligible subscribers are entitled to lifeline telephone service. Eligible subscribers are defined as participants in the following programs administered by the State Department of Social and Health Services (DSHS): Aid to Families With Dependent Children; chore services; food stamps; Supplemental Security Income; refugee assistance; and Community Options Program Entry System (COPES). Each of these programs' means is tested by the Department. The Department will certify participants in these programs for lifeline assistance and renew eligibility annually.

Under the program, lifeline service consists of three components. First, the local exchange deposit is waived for eligible subscribers. Second, a 50% discount on service connection fees is mandated. In addition, the remaining portion of the connection fee must be expressly payable through installment payments. Eligible subscribers are allowed one deposit waiver and one discount on service connection fees per year. Third, the Commission is directed to set a threshold rate for lifeline service throughout the state. All companies with rates currently above the lifeline rate level will file a lifeline rate and offer the discounted service to eligible subscribers. Companies whose current rates are below the lifeline threshold need not file a rate component. Lifeline service is limited to one residential access line per eligible household.

—West Virginia: enacted legislation effective July 1, 1986, requiring telephone companies to provide Telephone Assistance Service to low-income residential customers. Subscribers must be either disabled or at least 60 years of age and be receiving Social Security Supplemental Security Income benefits, Aid to Families With Dependent Children (AFDC) benefits, Aid to Families with Dependent Children-Unemployed (AFDC-U) benefits, food stamps, or be a member of a household whose total income qualifies under Social Security supplemental income programs. The state assistance at least matches the $2-per-month usage charge.

Notes

INTRODUCTION

1. The U.S. Department of Energy, Fuel Oil Marketing Advisory Committee, "Low-Income Energy Assistance Programs: A Profile of Need and Policy Options" (Washington, D.C., July 1980), p. 24.

2. U.S. Senator Edward M. Kennedy, testimony before the Fuel Oil Marketing Advisory Committee of the U.S. Department of Energy (Washington, D.C., August 10, 1979).

CHAPTER 1

1. Office of the White House Press Secretary, "The President's National Energy Efficiency Program: Phase Two," July 22, 1980.

2. Cleveland State University, College of Urban Affairs, "Energy Assistance Programs and Pricing Policies in the Fifty States to Benefit Elderly, Disabled, or Low-Income Households," prepared for the Ohio Energy Credits Advisory Committee (Cleveland, 1979).

3. Cleveland State University, College of Urban Affairs, "Energy Assistance Programs in the Fifty States, 1984, Survey Update" (Cleveland, 1985).

CHAPTER 2

1. Hans H. Landsberg and Joseph M. Dukert, *High Energy Costs, Uneven, Unfair, Unavoidable?* (Baltimore: Johns Hopkins University Press, 1981), p. 19.

2. U.S. Department of Health, Education and Welfare, "The Measures of Poverty, A Report to Congress as Mandated by the Education Amendment of 1974," April 1976, p. xxi.

3. Landsberg and Dukert, p. 19.

4. Lindsay Wright and Loren C. Cox, "The Impacts of Energy Price Increases on Low-Income Groups" (Boston: MIT Energy Laboratory, Working Paper, July 1980), p. 7.

5. "Poverty is More than Being Flat Broke," New York *Times,* April 1982 (interview with sociologist Peter Townsend).

6. Wright and Cox, p. 7.

7. Letter from Elsie Gerbhardt to Governor James Rhodes, April 1977.

8. These studies include: Eunice Grier and George Grier, "Too Cold—Too Dark, Rising Energy Prices and Low-Income Households" (Report to the Community Service Administration, 1978); Dorothy K. Newman and Dawn Day, *The American Energy Consumer* (Cambridge, Mass: Ballinger Press, 1975); Urban Institute, *The Distribution of Home Energy Expenditures by American Households in 1976-77: An Analysis of Energy Need Among Low-Income Groups* (Washington, D.C., May 1979); "National Survey of Household Energy Use" (Washington, D.C., Washington Center for Metropolitan Studies, 1975); U.S. Department of Energy, Fuel Oil Marketing Advisory Committee, "Low-Income Energy Assistance Programs: A Profile of Need and Policy Options" (Washington, D.C., July 1980).

9. Wright and Cox, pp. 1–3.

10. U.S. Department of Energy, Fuel Oil Marketing Advisory Committee (FOMAC), "Low-Income Energy Assistance Programs: A Profile of Need and Policy Options" (Washington, D.C., July 1980), p. 7.

11. Steven E. Ferry, "Solar Banking: Constructing New Solutions to the Urban Energy Crisis," *Harvard Journal on Legislation,* Summer 1981.

12. National Consumer Law Center, "Cold: Not By Choice, A State-By-State Analysis of the Impact of Energy Prices on the Poor, Elderly and the Unemployed," a report prepared with the assistance of the Grier partnership (Bethesda, Md., April 1984).

13. FOMAC, p. 2.

14. Lester C. Thurow, *The Zero Sum Society* (New York: Basic Books, 1980), p. 29.

15. Ibid., p. 31.

16. Bernard J. Frieden, "Household Energy Consumption: The Record and the Prospect," (Cambridge, Mass.: MIT Program on Neighborhood and Regional Change, 1981), p. 31.

17. U.S. Department of Health and Human Services, "Low-Income Home Energy Assistance Program," Report to Congress for FY 1983 to May 1985.

18. Eunice S. Grier, *Colder... Darker: The Energy Crisis and Low-Income Americans* (Washington, D.C.: Community Services Administration, June 1977), p. 3.

19. Dorothy K. Newman and Dawn Day, *The American Energy Consumer* (Cambridge, Mass.: Ballinger, 1975), p. xxiv.

20. "Energy Costs and the Poor—A Policy Strategy," *Center for Community Economic Development Review,* Fall 1979, p. 2.

21. U.S. Congress, Office of Technology Assessment, *Residential Energy Conservation Working Papers, Volume II* (Washington, D.C.: United States Government Printing Office, April 1979).

22. The Urban Institute, "The Impact of Residential Energy Conservation Standards on Households" (Washington, D.C.: Department of Commerce, National Technical Information Service, June 1980), p. 38.

23. Mark N. Cooper, Theodore L. Sullivan, Susan Punnett, and Ellen Berman, *Equity and Energy: Rising Energy Prices and the Living Standards of Lower Income Americans* (Boulder, Colo.: Westview Press, 1983), p. 7.

24. Frieden, p. 18.

25. Ibid., p. 21.

26. U.S. House of Representatives, Committee on Energy and Commerce, *Energy and the Elderly,* Sourcebook (Washington, D.C.: U.S. Government Printing Office, 1981), p. 33.

27. Frieden, p. 25.

28. Ibid., p. 29.

29. Robert Stobaugh and Daniel Yergin, eds., *Energy Future* (New York: Random House, 1979), p. 172.

CHAPTER 3

1. Ferry, p. 510.

2. U.S. Congress, Office of Technology Assessment, *Residential Energy Conservation Working Papers, Volume II* (Washington, D.C.: United States Government Printing Office, April 1979), p. 99.

3. Ibid., p. 104.

4. Sandra Evans Teeley, "Budget Cuts May be Bad Break for Housing," Cleveland *Plain Dealer,* February 21, 1982.

5. The Commonwealth of Massachusetts, Executive Office of Energy Resources, "Energy Conservation in Rental Housing," unpublished report, no date.

6. Cooper, Sullivan, Punnett, and Berman, p. 7.

7. OTA, p. 125.

CHAPTER 4

1. Lindsay Wright and Loren C. Cox, "Low Income Energy Assistance: Policy Alternatives and Recommendations" (Boston: MIT Energy Laboratory, Working Paper, March 1981), pp. 1–4.

2. Ibid., pp. 1–5.

3. U.S. Congress, Community Services Act of 1974, H.R. 14449, 93rd Cong., 2d Sess., 4 January 1975.

4. Ohio Weatherization and Home Energy Policy Advisory Committee, "Weatherization in Ohio" (Columbus, March 31, 1979), p. 22.

5. U.S. Department of Energy, *The Weatherization Assistance Program, Annual Report for 1980,* November 1980, p. 10.

6. Raymond J. Struyk, "Home Energy Costs and the Housing of the Poor and the Elderly," in *Energy Costs, Urban Development and Housing,* edited by Anthony Downs and Katherine L. Bradbury (Washington, D.C.: The Brookings Institute, 1984), p. 61.

7. Ferry, p. 488.

8. Ibid., p. 505.

9. Ibid., p. 508.

10. *Federal Register* 47, no. 42 (March 3, 1982), p. 9104.

CHAPTER 5

1. W. T. Gormley Jr., *Politics of Public Utility Regulation* (Pittsburgh: University of Pittsburgh Press, 1985), p. 14.

2. Ibid., p. 26.

3. Cleveland State University, "Energy Assistance Programs . . . 1984 Survey Update."

4. National Consumer Law Center, *Update* (Washington, D.C.: NCLC, March 22, 1982), p. 4.

5. Ibid., p. 4.

6. Ibid., p. 17.

7. *Journal of Housing,* December 1981, p. 600.

CHAPTER 6

1. Dr. Lance C. Buhl, Office of Corporate Contributions, Standard Oil Company, Cleveland, Ohio, telephone interview, 18 February 1986.

2. Carol A. Whitcomb and Maryann K. Moskiewicz, "Cutbacks: Tapping New Resources," *Public Welfare,* Winter 1982, p. 22.

3. "Foundations Decrease as Tax Benefits Fade," Cleveland *Plain Dealer,* August 16, 1985.

4. "Cleveland Receives Ford Grant . . . ," *Neighborhood Development,* Winter 1981–82, p. 1.

5. Cleveland State University, College of Urban Affairs, *Energy and the Poor: Alternative Non-Rate Structure Programs,* May 1981, pp. 174–183.

6. "Corporate Giving Fails to Offset Cuts by U.S.," New York *Times,* February 15, 1985.

CHAPTER 7

1. *A Citizens Guide to Electric Utilities,* League of Women Voters Educational Fund, Washington, D.C., 1985, p. 6.

2. See Alfred E. Kahn, *The Economics of Regulation: Principles and Institutions,* Vol. 1 (New York: John Wiley, 1971) for a discussion of utility pricing and economics.

3. Susan M. Shanaman, "Uncollectibles: An Issue for the Eighties," *Public Utilities Fortnightly,* May 13, 1982.

4. American Gas Association, *Gas Industry Manual,* Washington, D.C., p. 2.

5. Edison Electric Institute, Low- and Fixed-Income Energy Assistance Manual, Washington, D.C., November 1981, p. III-2.

6. For an inventory of innovative programs, see Cleveland State University, "Energy Assistance Programs, 1984 Survey Update," Chapter 6.

7. For a detailed description of state disconnect/reconnect policies, see Cleveland State University, College of Urban Affairs, "Disconnect Policies in the Fifty States, 1984 Survey," 1984.

8. National Association of Credit Managers (NACM), "A Compendium of Low-Income Assistance Programs," presented at the 89th Annual NACM Credit Congress, Washington, D.C., May 1985.

9. Technical Development Corporation, (TDC), "A Report for the Ford Foundation, An Evaluation of Energy Conservation Programs Serving Three Low-Income Neighborhoods: Overcoming the Barriers" (Boston: TDC, May 1985), p. 38.

10. Ibid., p. 23.

CHAPTER 8

1. Title I, Section II, *The Communications Act of 1934, As Amended,* 47 U.S.C. S 151.

2. U.S. Congress, Joint Hearings, Committee on Commerce, Science, and Transportation, U.S. Senate, and the Committee on Energy and Commerce, U.S. House of Representatives, *Universal Telephone Service Preservation Act of 1983,* 98th Cong., 1st sess. S. Hrg. 98-253 (Washington D.C.: U.S. Government Printing Office, 1983).

3. Letter from Robert D. Orr, chairman of Universal Telephone Service Task Force, to the Honorable Joseph E. Brennan, governor of Maine, August 19, 1983.

4. *Ohio Report,* Gongwer News Service, Inc., Volume 56, Report No. 188, September 29, 1983.

5. Schneidewind-UTSPA Testimony.

6. U.S. Supreme Court Justice Potter Stewart, in Jacobellis v. Ohio, *United States Reports,* Vol. 378 (Washington, D.C.: U.S. Government Printing Office, 1965), p. 197.

7. U.S. Congress, Joint Hearings, p. 118.

8. U.S. Congress, House, Committee on Energy and Commerce, *Report of the Committee on Energy and Commerce on H.R. 4102.* 98th Cong., 1st sess.

Report No. 98–479 (Washington, D.C.: Government Printing Office, 1983).

9. Ibid., p. 2.

10. U.S. Congress, Joint Hearings, p. 72.

11. Ibid., p. 73.

12. Congressional Budget Office, *The Changing Telephone Industry: Access Charges, Universal Service and Local Rates* (Washington, D.C.: U.S. Government Printing Office, 1984).

13. The Urban Center Energy Program, "Trends Report of Energy Assistance Programs in the Fifty States, 1979–1984." (Cleveland State University, College of Urban Affairs, 1985).

14. U.S., Congress, House, p. 56.

15. Congressional Budget Office, p. 35.

16. California Public Service Utilities Commission, Universal Lifeline Service Section 84–06–11, July 28, 1984.

17. *FCC News,* Report No. DC–260 (cc Dockets 78–22, 80–286), October 11, 1985.

18. *Bulletin,* National Association of Regulatory Utility Commissioners, NARUC NO. 11–1987, March 16, 1987, p. 21.

19. Statement by Bert Halpern, FCC representative to NARUC's Committee Communications, February 24, 1985, Washington, D.C.

20. The FCC charge in depreciation methodology has been a critical and little-understood issue both in terms of enabling the telephone companies to take advantage of rapidly improving new technologies as well as a major source of local service rate increases. Concern has been expressed in congressional hearings related to the FCC's approval of rapid changes in the depreciation schedules, which will net telephone companies $3.6 billion from their customers. The FCC has defended this action by stating:

If we had not taken this corrective action, the carriers' books of accounts would eventually have exhibited large reserve deficits for plant that was no longer in service. Future rate payers would have been required under rates and regulation, to pay a return on a nonexistent plant. This is clearly unacceptable and is inconsistent with depreciation accounting principles which call for the complete recovery of invested capital over the life of the asset.

See FCC Authorization Legislation Oversight Hearing before the Subcommittee on Telecommunications, Consumer Protection and Finance, U.S. House of Representatives, 98th Cong., Serial No. 98–25, (Washington, D.C.: U.S. Government Printing Office, April 19, 1983), p. 106.

21. It should be noted that historically, residential rates have generally been below cost. The subsidized lifeline rate would be in addition to any below-cost rate existing for the entire residential customer class.

22. Lester D. Taylor, *Telecommunications Demand: A Survey and Critique* (Cambridge, Mass.: Ballinger, 1980).

CHAPTER 9

1. Thomas C. Schelling, "Energy and Poverty," in *High Energy Costs: Assessing the Burden,* ed. Hans H. Landsberg (Washington, D.C.: Resources for the Future, 1982), p. 389.

2. J. H. Standish, V. M. McDonald, R. R. Meyers, and D. C. Sweet, *Trends Report of Energy Assistance Programs in the Fifty States,* 1979–1984, The National Regulatory Research Institute, Occasional Paper No. 11, December 1985.

3. National Consumer Law Center, "LIHEAP Participation Rates, Funds Per Participating Households and Cost Exposure," Washington, D.C., 1 January 1986.

4. Mark N. Cooper, "Conceptualizing and Measuring the Burden of High Energy Prices," in *High Energy Costs: Assessing the Burden,* ed. Hans H. Landsberg (Washington, D.C.: Resources for the Future, 1982), pp. 43–59.

5. Paul W. Barkley, "The Impacts of Rising Energy Prices in Rural Areas," High Energy Costs: Assessing the Burden, ed. Hans H. Landsberg (Washington, D.C.: Resources for the Future, 1982), p. 282.

6. U.S. General Accounting Office, *Slow Progress and Uncertain Energy Savings in Program to Weatherize Low-Income Households,* Report to Congress EMD 80–59 (May 15, 1980).

7. National Regulatory Research Institute, *Trends in State Regulatory Commission Development and Functioning,* The Ohio State University, Columbus, Ohio, 1979.

8. Standish, McDonald, Meyers, and Sweet.

9. Gar Alperovitz, "Informal Remarks on 'High Energy Costs: Assessing the Burden,'" in *High Energy Costs: Assessing the Burden,* ed. Hans H. Landsberg (Washington, D.C.: Resources for the Future, 1982), p. 402.

CHAPTER 10

1. Denis P. Doyle and Terry W. Hartle, *Excellence in Education—The States Take Charge,* (Washington, D.C.: American Enterprise Institute for Public Policy Research, 1985), pp. vii–viii.

2. Richard P. Nathan and Fred C. Doolittle, "The Untold Story of Reagan's New Federalism, *The Public Interest,* Fall 1984, p. 97.

3. Ibid., p. 101.

4. David C. Sweet, "New Federalism Will It Work?" speech delivered to Building Partnerships: Older Americans and Their Energy Suppliers, Washington, D.C., February 5, 1982.

5. John J. Gilligan, speech before the U.S. Congress, Joint Economic

Committee, 92 Cong., 1st sess., 25 January 1971, Congressional Information Service, microfiche.

6. Ronald Reagan, *State of The Union Message to a Joint Session of Congress,* 26 January 1982, in *Congress and the Nation,* Vol VI, ed. Mary W. Cohn (Washington, D.C.: Congressional Quarterly, Inc., 1985), Appendix, p. 1048.

7. Nathan and Doolittle, pp. 102–103.

8. Mary Procter, "The Impact on Regional Political Issues of Energy Price Increases," in *High Energy Costs: Assessing the Burden,* ed. Hans H. Landsberg (Washington, D.C.: Resources for the Future, 1982), p. 333.

9. Richard H. K. Vietor, *Energy Policy in America Since 1945: A Study of Business Government Relations* (New York: Cambridge University Press, 1984), p. 312.

10. R. Edward Freeman, "Managing the Strategic Challenge in Telecommunications," *Columbia Journal of World Business,* 18 (Spring 1983).

11. Ibid., p. 11.

12. Ibid., p. 11–12.

13. Freeman, p. 16.

14. Editorial, "Is Divestiture Working?" Cleveland *Plain Dealer,* September 1985.

15. Miller-Warren Energy Lifeline Act of 1975, Chapter 1010 of the Statutes of 1975, State of California, p. 2388.

16. Energy Credits Advisory Committee, *Energy Pricing Alternatives,* A Report to the Ohio General Assembly, Vol. 2, 1979, p. 4.

17. Richard D. Reinking, "Lifeline Telephone Service is a Reasonable Utility Classification," *Public Utilities Fortnightly,* July 25, 1985, p. 35.

18. Ibid., p. 35.

19. Ibid., p. 36.

20. Ibid., p. 37.

21. Sheldon W. Stabil, "The Emergent Telecommunication Revolution," *Midwest Focus,* Midwest Research Institute, Kansas City, Mo., May 1984, p. 1.

22. See David C. Sweet, "Demand Forecasts by the Electric Utility Industry: Fact or Fiction," *Proceedings,* Workshop on Long Run Energy Demands, The Mitre Corporation, Rosslyn, Virginia, May 1977.

23. David C. Sweet and David E. Jones, "Capital Conservation in the Electric Utilities," *Bulletin of Business Research,* The Ohio State University, Columbus, Ohio, November 1977.

24. See Alfred E. Kahn, *The Economics of Regulation: Principles and Institutions,* Vol. 1 (New York: John Wiley, 1971) for a discussion of utility pricing and economics.

25. V. Louise McCarren, "Funding the Future of the Telecommunications Industry: Managing Technological Innovation to Satisfy Consumer Demands," paper presented at Rensselaer Polytechnic Institute, Saratoga Springs, New York, June 3–5, 1985, p. 5.

26. Letter from Alfred E. Kahn, professor of political economy at Cornell University, to David C. Sweet, dean of the College of Urban Affairs at Cleveland State University, March 1987.

27. Alfred E. Kahn, "The Theory and Application of Regulation," *Antitrust Law Journal,* Spring Meeting Issue, 1986, p. 182.

28. Letter from Harry M. Trebing, director of the Institute of Public Utilities and professor of economics at Michigan State University, to David C. Sweet, dean of the College of Urban Affairs at Cleveland State University, March 1987.

29. Douglas N. Jones, "A Perspective on Social Contract and Telecommunications Regulation," monograph, The National Regulatory Research Institute, Columbus, Ohio, June 1987, p. 21.

Selected Bibliography

Allen, Edward H. *Handbook of Energy Policy for Local Governments.* Lexington, Massachusetts: Lexington Books, 1975.

The American Assembly, Columbia University. *Energy Conservation and Public Policy.* New Jersey: Prentice Hall, 1979.

Booz, Allen and Hamilton, Inc. *Alternative Metering Practices–Implications for Conservation in Multifamily Residences.* Report prepared for the U.S. Department of Energy, June 1979.

_____. *Utility Sponsored Home Insulation Programs.* Report prepared for the U.S. Department of Energy–Economic Regulatory Administration, June 1978.

Commoner, Barry, Howard Boksenbaum, and Michael Corr, eds. *Energy and Human Welfare–A Critical Analysis, Vol. III.* New York: MacMillan Information.

Cooper, Mark N., Theodore L. Sullivan, Susan Punnett and Ellen Berman. *Equity and Energy: Rising Energy Prices and the Living Standards of Lower Income Americans.* Boulder: Westview Press, 1983.

Daneke, Gregory A. and George K. Lagassa. *Energy Policy and Public Administration.* Lexington, Massachusetts: Lexington Books, 1980.

Danielson, Michael N., M. Hershey, and John M. Bayne. *One Nation, So Many Governments.* Lexington, Massachusetts: Lexington Books, 1977.

Downs, Anthony and Katherine L. Bradbury, eds. *Energy Costs, Urban Development and Housing.* Washington, D.C.: The Brookings Institute, 1984.

"Energy Costs and the Poor–A Policy Strategy." *Center for Community Economic Development Review,* Fall 1979.

The Energy Project. *New Initiatives in Energy Legislation: A State by State Guide: 1979–1980.* Prepared for the Conference on Alternative State and Local Policies, 1980.

Ferry, Steven. "The Ghosts of Cold November: An Examination of HUD's Energy Conservation Policy for the Poor." *The Clearinghouse Review,* May 1977.

_____. "Energy Needs of the Poor: A Saga of Ongoing Legislative Neglect and Local Abuse." *The Clearinghouse Review,* August 1977.

Fisher, Roger and William Ury. *Getting to Yes: Negotiating Agreement Without Giving In.* Boston: Houghton Mifflin, 1981.

The Ford Foundation. *Energy–The Next Twenty Years.* Cambridge, Massachusetts: Ballinger Publishing Company, 1979.

Freedberg, Michael and Hatfield, Anne. *Financing Energy Conservation: What states and cities can do.* The Conference on Alternative State and Local Policies, Washington, D.C. 1983.

Freeman, R. Edward. *Stakeholder Management and Industrial Marketing.* Minneapolis: Strategic Management Research Center, 1984.

Frieden, Bernard J. "Household Energy Consumption: The Record and the Prospect." Cambridge, Mass: MIT Program on Neighborhood and Regional Change, 1981.

Garn, Harvey A. and Wayne Lee Hoffman. "The Distribution of Home Energy Expenditures by American Households in 1976–77: An Analysis of Energy Need Among Low-Income Groups." The Urban Institute, 1979.

General Accounting Office. "Slow Progress and Uncertain Energy Savings in Program to Weatherize Low-Income Households." A report to the Congress of the United States, EMP–80–59, May 15, 1980.

Gormley, W. T., Jr. *The Politics of Public Utility Regulation.* Pittsburgh: University of Pittsburgh Press, 1983.

Grier, Eunice S. *Colder... Darker: The Energy Crisis and Low-Income Americans.* Washington, D.C.: Community Servcies Administration, June 1977.

A Guide to: State Energy Assistance Office, 1984. American Association of Retired Persons, Washington, D.C., December 1983.

Hudder, John J. "Low-Income Families and High Energy Costs–An Economic Study." Syracuse Research Corporation, September 1978.

Kannan, Narasimhan. *Energy, Economic Growth, and Equity in the U.S.* New York: Praeger Publishers, 1979.

Landsberg, Hans H. and Joseph M. Dukers, eds. *High Energy Costs, Uneven, Unfair, Unavoidable?* Baltimore, Johns Hopkins University Press, 1981.

Lawrence, Robert, ed. *New Dimensions to Energy Policy.* Lexington, Massachusetts: Lexington Books, 1979.

Manaster, Kenneth A. "Energy Equity for Poor: The Search for Fairness, in Federal Energy Assistance Policy." *The Harvard Environmental Law Review,* Volume 7, No. 2, 1983:371–427.

National Consumer Law Center Inc., with the Assistance of the Grier Partnership. *"Cold—Not by Choice, a State-by-State Analysis of the Impact of Energy Prices on the Poor, Elderly and the Unemployed."* Washington, D.C., April 1984.

Newman, Dorothy K. and Dawn Day. *The American Energy Consumer.* Cambridge, Massachusetts: Ballinger Publishing Co., 1975.

Office of Technology Assessment, U.S. Congress. *Residential Energy Conservation.* U.S. Government Printing Office, 1979.

Reisner, Robert A. F. *Energy Conservation and Public Policy.* Englewood Cliffs, New Jersey: Prentice Hall, Inc., 1979.

Stein, Ted. *The Path Not Taken: A Common Cause Study of Energy Conservation Programs.* Washington, D.C.: Common Cause, 1980.

Stern, Paul C.; J. Stanley Black; Julie T. Elworth. *Home Energy Conservation: Programs and Strategies for the 1980s.* The Institute for Consumer Policy Research, Consumers Union Foundation, Mount Vernon, New York, 1981.

Stobaugh, Robert and Daniel Yergin, eds. *Energy Future.* New York: Random House, 1979.

Technical Development Corporation. "A Report for the Ford Foundation, An Evaluation of Energy Conservation Programs Serving Three Low-Income Neighborhoods: Overcoming the Barriers." Boston: TDC, May 1985.

The U.S. Department of Energy, Fuel Oil Marketing Advisory Committee. "Low-Income Energy Assistance: A Profile of Need and Policy Options." July 1980.

Vietor, Richard H.K. "Energy Policy in America Since 1945: A Study of Business Government Relations." New York: Cambridge University Press, 1984.

Wright, Lindsay and Loren C. Cox. "The Impacts of Energy Price Increases on Low-Income Groups." Boston: MIT Energy Laboratory, Working Paper, July 1980.

Index

access charge, 94, 98, 102
access number (911), 104
ACTION program, 76–77
Action to Conserve Energy, 77
administration: coordination of, 5, 55, 122, 136; state costs of, 62
advisory councils, 39
Aid to Families with Dependent Children (AFDC), 3–8: direct aid to, 56; emergency payments, 38; RCAP and, 36–37. *See also* low-income households
Alabama Gas Company, 87
Alliance to Save Energy, 73
American Enterprise Institute, 126
American Gas Association, 80–81
American Red Cross, 83
American Society of Heating, Refrigeration and Air Conditioning Engineers (ASHRAE), 22
American Telephone and Telegraph Company (AT&T), 91; anti-trust suits, 94; competitors, 132; divestiture and, 96; subscriber plant costs, 99–101
Amoco Foundation, 75
Annual Housing Survey, Bureau of the Census, 19, 25
appliances, efficiency of, 15
Arkansas Public Utility Commission, lifeline, 109

audits, energy, 45: neighborhood programs, 77, 85; local government and, 65; RCS, 84–85; state policy and, 6

Baltimore Energy Alliance Program, 87
Baltimore Gas and Electric Company, 87
Baroody, William, Jr., 126–27
basic energy service, 54–55
Basic Measured Service rate, 113
billing plans, 81
Block grants (CDBG), 4, 36–38, 43, 51, 65

California, Energy Lifeline Act, 57, 104, 134
Carter administration, 3–4, 34
caulking, 20, 65, 87
Chicago Community Trust, 75
cities, 73; energy offices, 30; pricing patterns, 25
Citizens Conservation Corporation, 28
Civic Action Institute, 74
Cleveland Foundation, 76
Cleveland Plain Dealer, 94, 132
Cleveland State University: Center for Neighborhood Development, 74, 76; College of Urban Affairs Energy Program, 53, 123, Energy Program, 57, surveys, 56
Commercial customers, 5

communication, two-way, 131
Communications Act of (1934), 93
Comunity Action Agencies (CAAs):
    local governments and, 34–38,
    64–68; weatherization programs,
    39
Community Development Block
    Grants. *See* Block grants
community foundations, 73–76
Community Services Act, EECP and,
    35
Community Services Administration
    (CSA), 34–38
community foundations, 73–76
congress. *See* Federal government
Congressional Budget Office, 98
conservation programs, 3–4, 39;
    capital, 140; energy assistance
    programs and, 15–16, 122, 135,
    140; energy crisis and, 33; energy
    profits and, 53; grants for, 65;
    home improvement, 65; HUD
    programs, 43; incentives for, 21,
    43–44, 140; loans for, 65; low-cost
    utilities and, 80–81; low-income
    households and, 19–22; obstacles
    to, 18, 122; RCS, 44–45;
    rehabilitation programs, 65; rental
    units and, 28; standards, 28, 60,
    65; states and, 51; tax credits,
    43–44; use rates and, 47; utility
    programs, 84–85. *See also*
    weatherization; specific programs
conservation and renewable resource
    tax credits, 42
consumer expenditure survey, BLS, 11,
    13
Consumer Price Index (CPI), 14, 25
consumers, 33; basic rights of, 132;
    consumption patterns, 10, 15–25.
    See also specific sectors
cooling, costs of, 9
corporations: foundations, 71–73;
    strategy, 133. *See also* specific
    corporations
cost(s). *See* Energy prices
cost-effective energy standards, HUD,
    43

Council on Foundations, Yale
    University, 73
Cox, Loren C., 8, 33
crisis assistance projects, 7, 35–36, 39,
    56
Crisis Intervention Program (CIP),
    35–36, 56
crude oil: domestic decontrol of, 36,
    115; embargo (1973), 91, 115;
    production controls, 33. *See also*
    oil prices
Crude Oil Windfall Profits Tax Act
    (1980), 72
customers. *See* Consumers

degree-days, defined, 9
Department of Agriculture, 7
Department of Energy (DOE), 4–5;
    Fuel Marketing Advisory
    Committee, 4, 37, 67. *See also*
    specific programs
Department of Health and Human
    Services, 15, 36–37. *See also*
    specific programs
Department of Labor, BLS: Consumer
    Expenditure Survey, 11, 13;
    poverty measure, 8
deprivation index, 8
deregulation, 133
Dingle, John, 98
direct assistance programs, 3, 5, 56–59;
    AFDC and, 3–8, 38, 56–57;
    conservation and, 136; federal,
    35–42; funding of, 41, 58, 60;
    state components, 55, 57–60;
    targeted, 138; utilities and, 81, 83;
    weatherization and, 136
discrimination, 139
divestiture, 96, 125, 132
DOE. *See* Department of Energy
do-it-yourself kits, 65, 87

East Ohio Gas (EOG) Company, 15
Economic Opportunity Act (1964), 35
Economic Recovery Act (1981), 73
Edison Electric Institute, 80–81
educational programs, 65
elderly, 4, 9, 12

eligibility: LIHEAP and, 37–38; lifeline
    rates and, 47; measures of, 7–9;
    weatherization programs and, 39
Emergency Energy Assistance Program
    (EEAP), 35–36, 56
Emergency Energy Conservation
    Program (EECP), 35
Emergency Petroleum Allocation Act
    (1973), 33
energy assistance programs, 3–5;
    CAAS and, 64; constituencies, 4,
    96; consumption and, 15–16;
    crisis orientation of, 5, 8–9;
    decentralization and, 4, 64, 121;
    ECAP, 36–37; EEAP, 35–36, 56;
    emergence of, 34–42, 119; goals
    in, 4; as income, 8, 67;
    independent sector, 71–78; policy
    lessons of, 118–24, 136; public
    utilities and, 79–88; state, 5,
    51–68. See also federal
    government; specific programs
Energy Assurance Program, 55
energy audits. See audits, energy
Energy Bank, Minnegasco, 87
Energy Conservation Funds (ECFs), 75
Energy Conservation and Production
    Act (1976), 39
energy crisis, 5, 7–10, 91; decrease in,
    66; escalation of, 36–37; fossil
    fuels, 60; price controls and,
    33–34, 135; real income effects, 14
Energy Crisis Assistance Program
    (ECAP), 36–37
energy efficiency standards, 21
energy policy. See specific acts,
    programs
energy prices, 7–10, 66, 91;
    conservation incentives and,
    21–22; controls, 33–34;
    disruptions, 119; distributional
    effects of, 15; elasticity, 9; home
    energy, 9–12; housing
    abandonment and, 29; indirect, 9;
    as percentage of income, 10–14;
    price controls, 33–34, 135. See also
    energy crisis; specific problems
Energy Security Act (1980), 43

Energy Tax Act (1978), 44
entitlement benefits, 33, 48
excise tax, telephone usage, 138
Exxon Corporation, 77

Farmer's Home Administration
    (FMHA), 27, 40
faucet flow restrictors, 87
Federal Communication Commission
    (FCC): access charges, 94, 98–99,
    102; deregulation/divestiture
    decision, 132; local service rates
    and, 91
Federal Energy Administration (FEA).
    See Department of Energy
Federal government, 33–48; ATT
    divestiture and, 97; energy
    assistance policy, 4, 115, 125, 136,
    138; energy rates and, 91; funding
    by, 4–5, 41 (see also block grants);
    House Committee on Energy and
    Commerce, 98; Joint Lifeline
    Board, 109; minimum benefit
    and, 119; National Energy Plan
    34; policy coordination, 5;
    program cuts, 4, 48; shift in
    policy, 117; threats to, 94. See also
    New Federalism; specific agencies,
    programs.
Federal Housing Administration (FHA)
    standards, 16–17, 22
Ferry, Steven, 44
fixed income households, 4, 9, 12. See
    also specific groups
Florida Public Service Commission, 94
food stamp programs, 3, 8
Ford Foundation, 65, 74, 76
Ford Motor Company, 73
fossil fuel shortages, 60
foundations, 72–76
Fowler, Mark S., 98
Freeman, R. Edward, 130
Freiden, Bernard J., 15
fuel cooperatives, 65
fuel expenditures. See energy prices;
    income household
fuel oil. See Crude oil

Fuel Oil Marketing Advisory
  Committee (FOMAC), DOE, 4,
  37, 67
funding, 4–5, 41, 71–78, 83. *See also*
  specific government entity,
  program

gasoline costs, 9. *See also* oil prices
General Accounting Office, 122
General Assistance (GA), 38, 56, 135
General Motors Foundations, 73
George Gund Foundation, 74, 76
Gerbhardt, Elsie, 9
Gilligan, John J., 127–28
Gramm-Rudman Act, 127
grants: federal (*see* block grants); local,
  62, 65

Harvard University, Kennedy School of
  Government, 117
health care costs, 11
heating, 25; condition of systems, 21;
  residential, 5, 9, 16, 25; season, 5.
  See also specific fuel
Hipp, Edward, 97
home improvement, loan programs,
  62, 65. *See also* rehabilitation
Home Insulation Promotion Financing
  Program, 86
households: eligibility and, 7–9, 37–39,
  47, 139; Food Consumption
  Survey, 7; poverty indexes, 7–8.
  See also specific categories
housing stock: abandonment of, 18,
  29–30, 74; codes, 22; condition of,
  9; energy-efficient stock, 16;
  filter-down concept, 17; inflation
  of costs, 26; national energy goals
  and, 20; new construction, 28,
  42–43; RSC audits, 84–85;
  subsidized, 8, 27; urban, 25;
  vouchers and, 28. *See also*
  rehabilitation
Housing and Urban Development
  Department (HUD), Solar Bank,
  63. *See also* specific agencies,
  programs
hydroelectric power, 85

incentives, 21; in rental housing, 28;
  tax credits, 43–44. *See also* specific
  programs
income, household, 7–9; energy
  assistance as, 57; energy portion
  of, 10–14; in-kind benefits, 8;
  maintenance program, 7, 37;
  PIPP, 15, 55, 82; purchasing
  power of, 8, 14; redistribution of,
  78, 123; transfer program, 36–37
Independent sector programs, 71–78.
  See also specific programs
Indianapolis Foundation, 74
industrial customers, 5
Inflation, U.S., 92; energy-fueled, 7,
  26; income lag, 12
in-kind benefits, 8, 11, 27
insulation, 15; Home Insulation
  Promotion Financing Program, 86;
  income and, 19; low-income
  residents and, 87; standards for,
  16–17, 22. *See also* Conservation;
  weatherization program
interstate carriers, local exchange and,
  99–102

John A. Hartford Foundation, 74
Joint Lifeline Board, 110
Leisner, Susan W., 94
libraries, information programs, 136
life-line service rates, 18, 45; equity
  and, 46, 139; failure of, 120;
  revenue recovery and, 47; state
  programs, 46, 54, 81; telephone,
  95, 101
Lifeline Service Fund, 102
Lifeline Telephone Service Act (1985),
  101
LIHEAP. *See* Low-Income Home
  Energy Assistance Program
load-management programs, 5
loans, 65, 88
lobbying, by interest groups, 34, 62,
  81
local government, 4, 25, 39;
  conservation incentives and, 22;
  as service provider, 64–68. *See*

also cities; community action agencies

longitudinal research, 127

Low-Income Home Energy Assistance Program (LIHEAP), 8, 118; appropriation for, 41; consumption and, 15–16; do-it-yourself kits and, 87; eligibility and, 37–38; as entitlement program, 48; fund substitution, 56; seasonal utility customers and, 82; state program, 118; weatherization funds, 67

Low-Income Home Energy Assistance Program, 37, 67

low-income households, 120, 141; conservation and, 5, 19–22; definition of, 7–10; federal role, 37, 66–67 (*see also* specific program); housing stock, 15–16; independent sector's role, 77; real income of, 4; as stakeholders, 136; states and, 136; tax credits and, 43–44

lower-living standard (LLS), 8

McKnight Foundation, 74

Main Demonstration Program, 46–47

market-pricing, 122

Massachusetts Institute of Technology (MIT), energy laboratory, 8

master-metering, 18

Medicaid programs, 8–9

Medicare program, 9

Michigan Public Service Commission, 54, 86, 95

Minnesota Home Improvement Grant program, 62

mortgages: availability of, 27, 63; defaults, 26

Mortgage Subsidy Bond Tax Act (1980), 63

multifamily dwelling units. *See* rental units

National Association of Regulatory Utility Comissioners (NARUC), 97, 102

National Consumer Law Center, 14, 44

National Energy Conservation and Policy Act (1978), 40, 44

National Energy Plan, 34

National Governors Association, 95–96, 98

National Housing Act (1934), 27

National Interim Energy Conservation Survey (NIECS), DOE, 19

natural gas, price decontrol, 117

Neblett, Richard, 77

Neighborhood Energy Audit Program, 84–85

neighborhood organizations, 76, 84–85, 136

New construction, 28, 42–43

New Federalism, 4–6, 63, 118; failure of, 126; stakeholder leadership, 129; states and, 125; *See also* Block grants

New York Trust, 75

Nixon administration, energy policy, 33, 39

no losses test, 86

nonprofit oranizations (NPOs), 75–76

North Carolina Public Utilities Commission, 97

Northern States Power Company, 88

Oak Ridge National Laboratory, 21

Office of Economic Opportunity. *See* Community Services Administration

Ohio Bell, 133

Ohio Department of Taxation, 62

Ohio Energy Credits (OEC) Program, 15, 55, 62, 116, 118, 137

oil prices: controls on, 33–34, 135; decontrol of, 36, 115; FOMAC, 4, 37, 67; overcharge funds, 41, 56, 58, 63; regional differences, 120; rise in, 14, 36; windfall profits, 55 72

Okagaki, Alan, 44

Okagaki, Ron, 44

Omnibus Budget Reconciliation Act (1981), 37, 41

Organization of Petroleum Exporting
  Countries (OPEC), 36
outreach centers, 122, 136

Pacific North West Bell (PNWB), 113
peak demand, 5
Percentage of Income Payment Plan
  (PIPP), 15, 55, 82
petroleum. See Crude oil
policy, energy. See specific act,
  program
poor persons. See Low-income
  households; poverty
Portland (Maine) Wood Fuel Co-op, 76
Potter, Stewart U.S. Supreme Court
  Justice, 96
poverty: class, 139; defined, 7, 9;
  index, 7–8; line above, 139; See
  also Low-income households
price controls, 33–34, 135
price elasticity, 9
private sector programs, 4, 71–78
Procter, Mary, 129
profits, conservation and, 140
public housing, 27–28, 43
public utilities: bill increases, 92; block
  rate structure, 18; collection
  procedures, 82–83; direct
  payments, 42; energy rates and,
  91; low-interest loan guarantees,
  88; programs of, 35, 79–84, 134,
  136–39; rate based, 140; RCS and,
  44–45, 84–85; shared
  responsibility of, 141; social
  responsibility of, 80; surcharges,
  27; uncollectable accounts, 80. See
  also specific utilities
Public Utility Commissions (PUCs), 53,
  111, 138; NARUC, 97, 102; Ohio,
  55, 133; Pennsylvania, 79;
  proceedings, 110; public
  intervention and, 54–55; PURP
  programs, 45, 51, 123
Public Utility Regulatory Policy Act
  (PURPA), 45, 51, 55, 123. See also
  lifeline service rates

rates: interruptible, 54; PURPA and,

45, 51, 55, 123; rate base utility,
  140; revenue recovery and, 47
RCS. See Residential Conservation
  Service Program
Reagan administration, energy policy,
  4, 8, 63, 66, 91, 125. See also
  New Federalism
regulatory bodies. See Public Utility
  Commissions; specific agencies
rehabilitation: assistance programs
  and, 77; federal housing policy
  and, 28; HUD standards, 42–43
rental housing, 17–18, 25;
  abandonment of, 29–30;
  affordability of, 27–29; tax credits
  and, 44; weatherization of, 40–41
research and development activities,
  local, 65
Residential Conservation Service
  program (1978), 42, 44–45, 51, 84
residential energy: direct consumption
  of, 9–10, 12, 15, 18; policy
  coordination, 5; rising costs, 7–10;
  state policy, 6. See also rental
  housing
Residential Energy Conservation
  Survey, (DOE), 9
Residential Energy Consumption
  Survey (DOE), 10
retrofit heating systems, 76–77
Rhodes, James, 9
Rockefeller Brothers Fund, 75
Rosenberg, William G., 86
rural areas, energy costs, 94, 121

Salvation Army, 83
Schelling, Thomas C., 117
Schneidewind, Eric J., 95
self-employed, 8
Senior Citizen Coalition, 132
senior citizens. See elderly; low-income
  households
service-delivery coordination, 5
service rates. See rates
Shanaman, Susan M., 79
single-family units. See residential
  housing
social service agencies, 75–76, 136

solar energy, 42–44
Solar Energy and Energy Conservation
    Bank, 42–43
Southern California Gas Company, 87
space heating, 15
Special Crisis Intervention Program
    (SCIP), 35–42, 56
Spratley, William A., 95
stakeholder concept, 130, 140–41
Standard Oil Company, 65, 72–73, 75
state governments: administration of
    programs, 54–55, 62; advisory
    committees, 67; block grants, 4,
    36, 38, 51, 66; coordinated
    administration, 55; direct
    assistance programs, 56–59;
    discretion of, 37; energy offices,
    54; fiscal constraints, 51; fuel
    funds, 83–84; future of energy
    programs, 63–64; Governors
    association, 95; lifeline rate
    programs, 46–47; local
    government and, 66; payment
    plans and, 82; policy reassessment
    by, 5–6, 134–35; rate relief and,
    46; resurgence, 127; tax
    incentives, 44; telephone service
    and, 102, 105; transfer of funds
    by, 41–42; weatherization/
    conservation programs, 61
stockholders, of energy resources,
    14–15
storm windows, 15, 20, 87
subsistence diet, 7
supplemental Security Income (SSI):
    energy costs and, 14; RCAP and,
    36–37
Sweet, David C., 111

taxes: hidden, 47; incentives, 43–44;
    windfall profits and, 55, 72
technical assistance, local, 65
Technical Development Corporation
    (TDC), 28
telephone service, 11; AT&T, 94–96,
    99–101, 132; basic, 96; cost of
    service philosophy, 111; crisis in,
    91, 93, 96; equipment, 103, 140;

lifeline framework, 99, 101–3,
    112; local, 102; stakeholders in,
    131; state response, 102, 105;
    time-of-day rates, 54; universal
    service, 92–99, 138; value of
    service philosophy, 111
Thurow, Lester, 14

underemployment, 4, 8
unemployment, 4, 14, 40
United Way of America, 77
Universal Service Board, 102
Universal Service Fund, 102
Universal Telephone Preservation Act
    (1983), 97–99
Universal Telephone Service Task
    Force, 95
Urban Development Action Grant
    (UDAG) Program, 43
Urban Energy Program, Standard Oil
    Company, 73
urban areas. See cities
Utilities. See Public utilities

Vail, Theodore, 93
vendor line-of credit programs, 138–39
Veteran Administration's (VA), Section
    1800 program, 27
Vietor, Richard, 129
volunteers, 76
voucher system, 28

Washington Utility and Transportation
    Commission, 112
weatherization assistance programs:
    CAAs and, 35; coordinated
    rehabilitation and, 17; DOE's
    annual report, 41; do-it-yourself
    kits, 65, 87; eligibility, 5; LIHEAP
    funds, 38–42; local role, 64–68;
    NPOs and, 75; payback period,
    21; public-private financing, 87;
    rationale for, 55; savings from, 22;
    state programs, 59–62. See also
    conservation
weather stripping, 20, 65
welfare, state offices, 57. See also
    specific programs

windows; caulking, 17; energy-efficient, 77

workshops, 65
Wright, Lindsay, 8, 33

About the Authors

DAVID C. SWEET, Dean of the College and professor of Urban Affairs at Cleveland State University, was instrumental in creating an ongoing research program to study and evaluate energy assistance alternatives for the poor and elderly. Since 1979, the College's Energy Program has conducted a series of national surveys and has published numerous reports under his direction—including *Trends Report of Energy Assistance Programs in the 50 States, 1979-1984.* Before joining the College in 1978, Dean Sweet was a commissioner of the Ohio Public Utilities Commission for four years. While commissioner, he served as chair of the National Association of Regulatory Utility Commissioners' Administration Committee, which led the effort to create the National Regulatory Research Institute at The Ohio State University, and he served as the first chairman of the Ohio Department of Economic and Community Development. From 1971-75, he served in the cabinet of Ohio Governor John J. Gilligan, first as director of the Department of Development and then as director of the Department of Economic and Community Development. During this period, he chaired the five-member Ohio Energy Commission—comprised of utility, consumer and legislative representatives—which provided the first energy policies for the state. Prior to entering state government service, he headed regional economic research programs at Battelle Memorial Institute in Columbus, Ohio. Dean Sweet holds a doctorate from The Ohio State University, a master's degree from the University of North Carolina, and an undergraduate degree from the University of Rochester.

KATHRYN W. HEXTER is a consumer and educational services representative for East Ohio Gas Company in Cleveland, Ohio. She recently took a one-year leave of absence from the company to direct a project—conducted by the College of Urban Affairs at Cleveland State University for the Ohio Public Utilities Commission—to study how the state can more efficiently administer programs for low-income utility customers. From 1980–82, she also worked at the College as a senior research associate for its Energy Program. There she was principal researcher and author of reports on: the evaluation of lifeline electric rates; surveys of state programs providing financial assistance, as well as aid for weatherization and conservation; descriptions of model energy assistance programs; and development of alternative state coordination options for Ohio. In addition, she authored a report on a state program administrators' evaluation of federal energy assistance programs. She holds a master's degree in city and regional planning from Harvard University and an undergraduate degree from Washington University in Saint Louis, Missouri.